KT-488-684

PENGUIN BOOKS

TELL EVERYONE ON THIS TRAIN I LOVE THEM

MAEVE HIGGINS is a writer whose work appears regularly in *The New York Times*, *The New York Review of Books*, and *The Guardian* (London). A New Yorker originally from Ireland, she is an NPR favorite and hosts a live comedy show each week in Brooklyn. In 2020, her starring role in the comedy-horror movie *Extra Ordinary* garnered acclaim around the world. Maeve's long-term goal is to own a donkey or two.

ALSO BY MAEVE HIGGINS

Maeve in America

Maeve Higgins

Tell Everyone on This Train I Love Them

Essays

PENGUIN BOOKS

PENGUIN BOOKS

An imprint of Penguin Random House LLC
penguinrandomhouse.com

LIBRARY OF CONGRESS CATALOGING-IN-PUBLICATION DATA
Names: Higgins, Maeve, author.
Title: Tell everyone on this train I love them: essays / Maeve Higgins.
Description: [New York] : Penguin Books, [2022] |
Identifiers: LCCN 2021044071 (print) |
LCCN 2021044072 (ebook) |
ISBN 9780143135869 (trade paperback) |
ISBN 9780525507444 (ebook)
Subjects: LCSH: Higgins, Maeve. |
Women comedians—United States—Biography. |
Women comedians—Ireland—Biography. |
Irish—United States—Biography. | Conduct of life—Humor.
Classification: LCC PN2287.H496 A3 2022 (print) |
LCC PN2287.H496 (ebook) |
DDC 824/.92—dc23/eng/20211101
LC record available at https://lccn.loc.gov/2021044071
LC ebook record available at https://lccn.loc.gov/2021044072

Printed in the United States of America
1st Printing

Set in Adobe Garamond Pro
Designed by Sabrina Bowers

"Amor mundi—warum ist es so schwer, die Welt zu lieben?"

"Love of the world—why is it so difficult to love the world?"
—*Hannah Arendt*

Contents

Lean on Me
1

Bubbles and Planks
19

Good Acting
41

Misneach and *Rumors of War*
57

Situational Awareness
85

Death Tax
113

The Innocents
141

New York, Fair or No Fair
171

Notes and Acknowledgments
205

Tell Everyone
on This Train
I Love Them

Lean on Me

My most fervent wish during the COVID-19 pandemic was twofold. One, that it end. Two, that it not impart any damn lessons. I can't stand when horrible and senseless things happen and people insist on finding some neat takeaway to make sense of it all. Despite my resistance to learning anything from this nasty demon of a virus, it did help crystallize one thing for me. You'll snort when you hear, because it's incredibly obvious. My realization was this: I really, really, REALLY need my friends. No man is an island; we all know this. Although for many years of my childhood I thought the expression was "No man is in Ireland" and it confused me greatly, particularly when said by a man in Ireland, but I still nodded wisely when I heard it. *So true, no man is in Ireland*, I would agree, my little eyes darting around in confusion.

I have one brother and six sisters, you see, and the thing about my siblings is that they count as friends too. I had no idea what that meant for my friendships with people who are not related to me until my friend Claudia told me exactly what it meant. "You don't really need friends because you have your family," she said. "Oh, I doubt that's true," I told her, knowing in an instant it was true. I was worried I'd hurt her feelings if I confirmed it. She smiled, knowing me well enough to spot a lie. "It's fine, Maeve, it's not a bad thing."

I wasn't always best friends with my siblings, certainly not as a child. I had running battles with both my older sister and my closest-in-age younger sister. My older sister was a stealth bomber, quieter and cleverer than I. When my family took a day trip to Midleton, a town thirty minutes' drive away, they accidentally left me behind. That day we spent a long time in a carpet shop. I was about six and I didn't notice the rest of my family leaving, immersed as I was in the swirling floral rugs of the 1980s. When I did notice, I couldn't believe it. I remember walking around the shop, through the long swinging halls of hanging carpet, unable to comprehend that they were all gone. Just like that, all those siblings and both parents had vanished. Because we were in the same classroom in the same school growing up, and we only really went on playdates together to cousins' houses, I'd never been without a family member before in my life. I decided to stand very still and hope nobody noticed me, convinced I would get in trouble with the shop owner for being there alone. Nobody noticed my presence in the shop, or my absence in the car. Well, eventually they did, otherwise I wouldn't be writing this book; I'd be the heiress to a rug fortune, having no doubt been adopted by the Carpet King of Midleton. As my family pulled into the driveway after a successful outing (no money spent, three hours passed, zero fights in the backseat) my mother realized I wasn't there. "Where's Maeve?" she asked. My nine-year-old sister replied, a little too calmly, "Oh, Maeve? She's back at the carpet shop." As if I was her interior designer and she'd left me there with her credit card to pick up a rug she was too busy to select.

As small girls she and I shared a room with our two younger sisters, sleeping in two sets of bunk beds. With an average of two years between us, I seem to remember we were all around the same size and we shared some clothes, like socks and underwear. We would fight about that, but she was always ahead of me in the smarts department. She learned how to spell first, a skill I was insanely jealous of. "*G.O.T.O.S.L.E.E.P.*," she would hiss when I wouldn't stop talking at nighttime, and I'd beg her to tell me what it meant. "Go to sleep," she'd say, and I'd promise to go to sleep if she'd just tell me what she had spelled. She was a high-achieving and extremely good child, doing everything she could think of to help our mother. This annoyed me, and I annoyed her. I was lazy and funny, like now. While she swept the stairs and looked after whatever baby needed looking after, I'd play outside and make my father laugh as I helped him shape concrete into bricks. It's really not advisable to have children handle concrete, what with the lime and all, but it was really satisfying work.

On Saturday mornings, my parents would go to the market in Cork to get supplies for the week, and it was my older sister's job to cajole us all into cleaning the house. "I'll polish," I'd offer, knowing that meant I could put on the television and half-heartedly wipe the plant pots and our only statue. That statue, inexplicably, was a small bronze figurine of a wolf suckling Romulus and Remus. "No, Maeve, you will clean out the fire." I hated cleaning out the fire; it involved various steps in turn irritating, grimy, and arduous. First the ashes would need to be roughly sieved so all the clinkers could be saved. Clinkers are the little bits of half-burned matter that would do well for the next fire. So, put the clinkers aside in a little pile and shovel out the ashes into a metal bucket. (Sometimes they were still very hot, adding an element of fear to the task.) This would inevitably leave your hands coated in a fine ashy dust that felt so gross to the touch it makes me shudder for a second at the mere memory. Then you'd have to bring the ash outside (yuck, outside!) and toss it into the ash heap, and load up on kippins (little sticks), wooden logs, turf, and coal to build a new fire. I dodged that whole job so often during the week that my sister always insisted it was my turn on Saturday, which it probably was. I'd make a long speech about parity and trust and how she was basically Miss Hannigan, and she would usually end up cleaning the fire.

As teenagers, my older sister and I still shared a room, and the younger ones had their own. This didn't really improve relations because we remained two people with extremely different personalities. If you're wondering what my "personality" was, what I mean is I would get home from school and make white toast, cover it in butter, and eat it lying on my bed, reading Louisa May Alcott books and humming tunelessly. For hours. Until dinner, which was often made by my older sister. Sometimes, when she had turned off the light and was trying to sleep, I'd come up with a plan exclusively to irritate her. I'd say, "I'm just going to say good night to my star," then I'd open the curtain and gaze silently at the sky for a really long time. I don't know how she resisted putting a pillow over my face.

My younger sister was a different type of threat. I resented being responsible for her, having learned early on that

I was. I was around five when we visited some family friends and we were playing around in their garden. They had a fat blond dog who, for some reason, took a dislike to Lilly. The dog chased her, and I remember her running past me with her two little braids streaming behind her. I knew it was bad, and I think I went to get an adult. The dog didn't bite her, but she was very frightened. I don't remember much else apart from later that evening, when I was punished for not looking after her. I found this deeply unjust, and complained to my mother that I didn't deserve a smack with the wooden spoon just because my little sister had been chased by a dog. My mother, with tears in her own eyes, was adamant that we must be loyal to one another, and protect and defend one another, and I had failed to do that.

So the loyalty is set, no matter what. I have these six girls, now women, and one boy, now man, that are mine. When it comes to sports teams, provincial rivalries, and even nation-states, I really don't care to identify with one or another, and feel faintly embarrassed for people who do. However, I know that if my brother and sisters needed me to paint my face or chant in a stadium or wave a flag to pledge my allegiance, I would happily do all of that. We grew up together, which sounds like a completely average thing to do, but is quite amazing when you break it down. Nobody else spent time pressed together in a pickup truck driving around to look at bridges my father liked, nobody else had to bear my teenage opining on East Timor's political situation, and nobody else believed me when I said I woke up while the dentist was pulling out four of my teeth. The time spent together, and the unconditional acceptance of one another that we built in our childhood, became a connection strong enough to withstand any amount of time or distance.

We are spread across the world now. Between us we rival the dating profile of a forty-year-old finance guy, with obscure flags lined up beside our names including Sweden, Mongolia, and the Central African Republic. I currently have siblings in the Middle East, in England, in Ireland—and then there is me, repping the Higgins name hard and alone in the United States. Our primary form of contact is a group WhatsApp chat: my parents and the eight children, just the ten of us. Every now and then one of us loses a phone or changes a number, and we start a new chat. The current one was created in August 2017 and holds ten thousand photos and probably four times as many messages.

When I wake up in New York there are messages from the Middle East, where my brother and one sister are eight hours ahead of me, waiting first; then the messages from Europe flood in from five hours in the future. Jokes and conversations are well underway as I make coffee and read the responses to the message I sent before I went to sleep: a photo of a pair of bronze and marble eyes from the fifth century I'd seen at the Met that day, captioned "me looking at dem scones." Bad news and difficult conversations are reserved for phone calls and visits. The WhatsApp group is chatter to let us know the small stuff, to keep us company wherever we are. It's this small stuff, these wispy threads, that weave seamlessly into a fabric that stretches over the time and space between us. I'm usually the last to check in on the family chat, from the subway coming home after a show or sun drunk after a trip to Brighton Beach. I read over the dozens of messages from the day, then I send photos of me posing with my head in a life-size Russian doll cut-out followed by a series of small bouncing pink heart emojis. It strikes me that the reason I'm able to be here in the US on my own, and have this life I love, is that my family set me up for it. How lucky that they made me strong enough to leave. From the next morning in Jordan, my sister sends the letters g.o.t.o.s.l.e.e.p.

Of course this isn't the case with everyone, but my family made me who I am. They've given me pretty much everything, every piece of the person who became me. Those pieces, just like Frankenstein's monster, were then animated—in my case, by the electricity of curiosity and ambition and independence—and I became my own person.

There were things I needed to go outside of my family to

get, and I believe I got those things from my friends. If I once saw my friends as bonus material in the film of my life, peripheral characters, it's because I failed to understand what central players they were until I was separated from them by COVID-19. In the 1931 film *Frankenstein*, there is an infamous scene of the monster getting overexcited by social contact and flinging Maria, his little friend, into a lake. I knew that I would be just the same way by the end of the isolation created by the pandemic. I would surely be so happy to see my friends I'd mutter and tremble with joy and more than likely I'd accidentally drown them. Still, I couldn't wait!

Aside from a snatched walk here and there or a chilly drink on a Brooklyn sidewalk, I didn't have any new experiences with my friends for many months. Instead, I turned over memories of old experiences with them like treasures found at the bottom of the ocean. At night I'd dive down and come back up with Thanksgiving night 2016. My friend Abi and her husband, Noel, rented chairs and made tables out of plywood, and almost twenty of us showed up. There was wine and music and huge platters of food we breathed over without a care in the world. I don't remember what we talked about, but I can see, clear as day, my friend Emilie on one side of the table and my friend Sophie on the other. There were some new, interesting people dotted around, and all of us were laughing our heads off. Maybe at something I said! As we laughed we passed the buttery mounds of pota-toes, like some corny scene in a holiday movie. That memory, and more like it, sustained me throughout the lockdown. I almost didn't go to Abi's that evening because all the pies were sold out at the bakery I went to, can you believe that? As if anyone cared, as if we needed anything more than each other and a warm place to sit and be together.

I grew up Catholic, and at the age of seven I was fervently told by a priest in a box that if I simply said half a dozen Hail Marys I'd be forgiven for being mean to my sister. "Deal," I said, smiling like the devil himself. During the pandemic, I heard myself bargaining with a different higher power. Science maybe, or government. "Please," I said out into the void. "Let all my friends get through this, and I swear I'll never cancel on them again." No matter what. Not for a date, not for a deadline, not even for my bulletproof millennial excuse, exhaustion. Like everyone in New York, my friends and I were scattered, both physically and men-tally. I swore that once everyone made it out the other side I would never leave their messages unread and I would always answer their calls. In the past when I've found myself at a low point that could last for weeks or months, it was man-ageable to fake feeling fine for the couple of hours that usually make up a friend date in the city. Coffee, a movie, drinks; these pleasant distractions can cover a multitude.

The pandemic stripped all of that away. Now I knew I'd be there when my friends were dull and downhearted with nothing much to say, and I knew it was fine to be that way. We didn't love each other any less.

The pandemic threw most of the building blocks of my life up in the air, including having a place to live. Luckily my friend Jon said I could stay in his apartment while he was with his family upstate. I FaceTimed him from his own living room to ask how to get red wine out of cream cushion covers and he said, "Stay for as long as you want, take whatever you need."

I discovered as I spent long spells alone during the pandemic that the liberation that comes with being alone in a new country turns easily to isolation—particularly in, well, isolation. I was sick of us all being lone bullfrogs on solitary lily pads, knowing how much better it feels to be part of a big croaking chorus carousing around the city. The loneliness drilled into me why we call it "making" friends; it's an effort and a choice and something that isn't ever really finished. Truly, though, I don't want to give that nasty little bug any credit. There was no silver lining or hidden meaning in it for me; I just really missed my friends.

Back in the 1990s, when I still had curly bangs and traces of optimism, a man named Robin Dunbar, a British anthropologist and researcher, observed a correlation between brain size and social relationships. Turns out the bigger an animal's brain is, the larger that animal's social group. If you're human (like me) your social sphere, meaning the number of people you're capable of holding in your brain, is around 150 people. Dunbar also looked at the emotional depth of those relationships and figured out that the closest emotional layer can contain just five individuals.

Around the same time Robin Dunbar was doing his research on brains and friends, the rest of us were setting our brains gently aside and fixating on a TV show called *Friends*. In *Friends*, their criterion for friendship was whiteness. I hope my rules are more complicated and less race based. I sit and think hard about who my top five friends are. I decide not to write down their names, in case I get that list mixed up with my list of enemies.

Examining my list of friends, I note that I veer toward people who are Aries and have brown hair and are women. You know, people like me. Is it unhealthy to surround myself with replicants? Does that make me a narcissist? Being practical now, I break down the types of friends who I could really use, like a rich friend who can serve as something of a patron. I'll call her Marina and I'll say to her, "Would you be a dear and fund this new podcast idea I'm developing? It's about badgers and whether or not they're emissaries to the Underworld. I need maybe . . . half a million." I need a friend who will marry me if my US visa gets canceled or if I feel like having a wedding but not a marriage. I need a friend who has read more than me so I can learn from them. Oh, and someone who's read less than me so I can show off to them. And I definitely need a friend who knows how to connect my phone to my laptop without a USB . . . but wait! All of this sounds far too transactional, even mercenary.

Every relationship is some kind of bargain, I suppose, but I'm not about to examine the reasons why someone would want to be friends with me. I must assume that every now and then, I am the right person at the right time, and am capable of saying or not saying whatever is needed in that moment. That's something that I love about my friends. Each one of them seems to pop up when I need them the most, with a thought or an action or a vibe that I didn't even know I needed. There are the big days like Thanksgiving, and the smaller days where they turn things around in a heartbeat.

One drizzly afternoon I was on my way to visit my friend Negin in the East Village and I stopped to take a selfie. I was texting with another friend about the new Hudson Yards building and placed my selfie'd face onto "the Vessel" so it looked like I was a benevolent God smiling down from the huge honeycomb structure. I was chuckling to myself as I sent off the image, when I heard a vicious voice shout, "YOU

BETTER NOT BE TAKING A PICTURE OF ME, YOU FAT WHORE!" I looked up, shocked, at the man who'd shouted. He shook his hand at me in a "get away, you pesky mosquito" kind of way and walked quickly on.

This all felt deeply unfair because I wasn't taking a photo of him. *Wait,* I wanted to say, *look! It's just a funny photo of me pretending to endorse these billion-dollar structures taking over the city!* I didn't say anything, though, because he was half a block away at that stage as well as quite enraged. But I have such a keen sense of justice when it comes to myself and I cannot bear to be accused of something I didn't do! Or even something I did! I trudged on, my good mood thoroughly dampened. It was clear from his tone that he meant "fat whore" in a bad way, as an insult. You may think being a fat whore would offer more value for money, but he was not in that headspace, not at all. He was trying to hurt my feelings!

I frowned as I buzzed Negin's apartment. How dare that stranger call me fat! That's just his opinion, albeit shared by my doctor and nutritionist. Besides, I'm fine with how fat I am. For a long time I was in a war with food and now I'm not. I've engineered a ceasefire. All weapons have been melted down and poured over nachos. It's peaceful now. In the elevator up to Negin's floor, I continued to grumble to myself. He shouldn't have said "whore." The correct term is "sex worker," and that part about me being a sex worker was not accurate. I don't have it in me to be a sex worker. Truly I would never have the patience, the skill, or the courage for that job. Overall I was upset at this stab of aggression that made a rent in the fabric of gentleness I'm accustomed to.

Negin greeted me at the door. She mouthed to me that she was on the phone, and I gestured I would use the bathroom. Inside, I looked at the mirror carefully, pressing my face into my neck to inspect my double chin and standing sideways puffing out and sucking in my tummy. I came out and joined her in the kitchen, where she was pulling some baby carrots and hummus out of the fridge for us to snack on. I told her what the man had shouted at me; I even did an impression that made him sound crueler. I did that by slowing down and really enunciating the words. "He turned to me and said you better NOT be taking a picture. You FAT. WHORE."

Negin rolled her eyes and continued rinsing the carrots. "Ugh, I hate when they do that."

I was not expecting that. "When they do . . . what?"

She tasted the hummus. "You know, when they yell at you on the street and call you names. I haven't heard 'fat' in a while; that seems to be a little less acceptable these days." She wandered away to put the tray on the coffee table and check on her sleeping baby. Her nonchalance was a revelation. I was fully expecting a face crumpled with out-rage and pity followed by an avalanche of comforting words. That is what my family would have done. Then I would have nursed my grievance and told the story again and again until it meant something, something much larger than the truth of what had happened, which was really just a guy crying out into the great nothing. Negin knew just what to say and do. She transmitted to me that what had happened wasn't personal and didn't matter. I went right back to chuckling, then joined her on the sofa. I was thinking, as we sat and I cuddled her baby and she talked about the Supreme Court, that I was lucky to be her friend.

I did have one pandemic friend date that I have put into that treasure box, in this case quite literally on the seabed. One Saturday morning in August 2020, my friend Mary drove us to the Rockaways over in Queens. Mary is a writer too, and like many New Yorkers she long eschewed cars in favor of public transport until the pandemic rendered the latter a health risk. So she rented a car and we got there be-fore the sun got too high in the sky and burned our skin. It was one of the hottest summers on record and became the year the climate crisis shifted New York into a humid sub-tropical climate zone. We set up a little camp with towels and a big umbrella, then stripped off and went straight into the maw of the great gray-green ocean. It's fun to sea swim with a friend for the first time. You see them in a new way, in a new element. Mary bobbed, laughing in a striped bathing suit. Just a few steps out, the water gets too deep to stand and you have to trust that it will hold you up, and it does. Back onto the beach to warm up, and then in again. By ten a.m. the lifeguard was clambering up onto his wooden seat and we were ready to leave. I always want to hear Mary, but what I listened to that morning was the quiet in the car home. I suppose we were just too calm to talk, to put a narrative on the experience, and isn't that a wonderful thing?

Bubbles and Planks

I was in Paper Source, looking at fancy paper and plastic chicks that lit up, when my arms began to feel really far away from my body. It was almost Easter, and I was halfway through a busy Tuesday, packing up an apartment I had been subletting and preparing to fly out of town for two months the next day. I was looking forward to leaving New York because I had been feeling quite shaky for a while, like I was standing in the dead center of the seesaw that is my brain, on one side high anxiety and the other deep depression. I could feel myself sliding but couldn't tell which way it would go this time. I was first diagnosed with depression when I was eighteen, but I've had it and its horrible little twin—anxiety—in me for much longer. Since then I've assembled a battalion of preventative measures that largely work. At that time, I was working constantly, hoping I could ward off whatever ugliness was waiting inside me by keeping busy. Sometimes that helps.

I had been assigning myself little tasks all day long, a technique I use to feel stressed and important. That morning I'd squeezed in a breakfast catch-up with a friend. She's a person I'm always meaning to see more often. We're not super close but I adore her and had recently learned that she had cancer. I wanted to see her before I left, to ask how she was doing, and fill her in on my news, of course. It can be hard to know what to say to a sick person, but I was finally watching *The Americans* and had just found out the romantic leads are a couple IRL and I had plenty of breathless opinions on that.

We had a good breakfast with great coffee and the kind of conversation I like best: one that veers healthily between meaningful and gossipy. We hugged good-bye, and she handed me a pretty little box of artisanal candy. I was mortified I hadn't brought her a gift, but she waved me off, saying it was just a regift and she hoped I'd enjoy them. I did; in fact, I was very glad of the candy when I got hungry around one-ish. My kitchen stuff was mostly packed away and the fridge was empty, so instead of making a sandwich or ordering in, I tore open the box. There was a fruit jelly that tasted delicious, although I couldn't make out exactly what the flavor was. I looked at the ingredients. Lychee fruit, that was it—yum! I happily bolted two of those and a peanut butter–chocolate concoction, a kind of chichi Snickers. Sometimes adults resist eating candy as a meal because they understand cause and effect. They do not want to experience the sugar rush followed by the inevitable sleepiness. I always power through, though, sometimes by cleverly eating even more candy a few hours later.

I'd arranged to meet another friend, Emmy, in the stationery store. She had yet to arrive when I first noticed how long my arms were. *This is extraordinary*, I thought, as I stretched my arms out and looked at my hands, which reached all the way across the store. On one wall were rows of thick, luxurious-looking cards. How funny, I thought, if I should crawl underneath a card and pretend it was a weighted blanket. But wasn't I much bigger than the card? Not sure actually, it seemed like my arms were much longer than I'd previously realized but my body was tiny and vulnerable. Although the cards were just at my fingertips I couldn't quite reach them, so while I laughed aloud to myself at the idea of crawling beneath one, I didn't actually try to do it. I decided instead to put a light-up chick in my mouth and make a short video of it illuminating the inside of my mouth. This tickled me to no end. I would put the video on Instagram and everyone would absolutely die. Oh, and I'd stand with my back to the door and when Emmy came in I'd spin around to face her with the chick flashing in my mouth and she would laugh and laugh, like I was laughing, quite hysterically.

I tried to pick up a chick but found I couldn't, because my hands were too far away. The flickering chicks and glittering bunnies gazed up at me, and I couldn't quite meet their eyes. I stopped laughing. What was I thinking? Why would I do such a thing? I wasn't the only one who wanted answers. I suddenly felt very keenly that the woman behind the register knew exactly what I had been plotting, and she was very angry with me. I stared at her. She was pretending to help another customer, acting as if she didn't even notice me. I hauled my arms back toward my body; they were ungainly now, having grown by approximately 30 percent. I folded them back up toward my body as best I could. I kept a close eye on the sales assistant. She was still playing the long game. She didn't even flinch. I left the shop as quickly as I could, which was not quickly at all because my legs had also grown, clunky and thick. I had to really concentrate on moving each foot, gradually making my way closer to the door.

Outside, I got as far away as I could from the store. I've lived in that neighborhood for years now, but nothing seemed familiar. I stayed very still and tried to find a landmark, but I could see nothing except hordes of viciously tall people, marching past, pushing these freaky-looking, much smaller people in strollers. I knew they were all judging me, especially those smaller ones with their big, staring eyes. They knew I was bad. It was too much; I turned to face the wall, which turned out to be the window of Paper Source, the place I thought I'd left far behind. I peered in, trying to see my little chick comrades. I couldn't focus, but I did catch sight of the woman behind the counter. She was wearing a cardigan and smiling, which is exactly what a spy would do. But why was she going to report me? Oh, yes, because I am fundamentally bad. But why did I think that? I tried to re-mind myself of something I hadn't ever known and that's when it hit me.

Resting my forehead on the window, a line from an Emily Dickinson poem boomed into my consciousness. "And then a plank in reason broke." That's what must have happened, my mind broke, just as my mother always feared it would. I've long known that I'm her favorite of eight children, be-cause ever since I was a little girl she's always told me it's *my* mental health she worries about the most. Now, here I was; a plank in reason had finally broken and I was falling down, and down. I wondered if I'd land, and if I did, where. With a family history of mental illness I knew firsthand that there was a range of places, and some of them were frightening.

I felt tears jumping in my eyes and couldn't calm myself.

Usually when I feel tears coming I can talk myself out of crying. I can just pop them on hold and reschedule them for a more convenient moment. Not this time. I was losing my mind and the ability to control my emotions. Luckily, my friend Emmy showed up. She is one of my favorites, both wry and equanimous. I cannot remember the first time we met, which makes sense because she's not a showy person, but a conversation is always better when she is in it. Sadly we weren't in a conversation now, but facing each other on a freezing cold street as I tried to form words with a completely dry mouth. "Something happened; it's my mind," I tried to say, but couldn't get the words out. Hopeless, I shook my head. Emmy looked carefully at my face and then told me that I looked like a cartoon of a stoned person. *Stoned?* I thought. But I don't smoke weed.

"Your eyes are completely ringed in red," she said, laughing. "Come on, let's get you home." With huge effort, I texted the friend who'd given me the candy. It was the last message I would send before it became impossible to use my phone for two days. I typed, "Was there something in the candy?"

The twenty-minute walk back to my apartment felt epic in scale. Emmy put a bottle of orange juice into my hands, but I couldn't do anything with it. My hands got colder and colder, but I couldn't explain that I didn't want to hold the juice. The step up a few inches from the road onto the sidewalk felt insurmountable, and I dealt with this by stopping and very deliberately lifting one leg at a time high into the air to make sure I didn't miss the curb. The railings lining the houses warped and roiled alongside me like living things.

I felt relief, even in that state. I was not having a breakdown! I was just incredibly high. I should have known, because the way my mental health, or rather mental illness, works is far slower and less conspicuous than a public snap. If I do end up losing my mind, it will be through a much longer process where I become so ground down by sadness and fear I will just kind of get quiet and fade out. Naturally, I resist that unhappy ending, and I am lucky enough to have a therapist and medication, and to know how best to look after my mental health by looking after my body and my relationships as best I can. But I understand that sometimes, as with all illnesses, a person isn't able to fight anymore. I'm glad to understand my mind a little more now than I once did. As a young teenager I was buffeted about terribly by what I thought were mere moods; I was frantic with self-loathing or I was sad about nothing or I was simply separated from my friends and family and the world by that thick pane of glass. Now, at the risk of sounding like a young teenager again, I had gotten used to the darkness inside me. I know that it comes from inside but is also an existential pain that is shared by many of us. So it made sense that what happened in Paper Source was not a real disintegration, just a temporary, chemically induced one, which I had brought upon myself by eating a whole box of weed candy for lunch.

I felt very far away, but with huge effort I could wrench myself back to Emmy and the task at hand: getting home. I was so grateful she was beside me, but every other person horrified me. They loomed too close and gazed too far into me. Fortunately Emmy led us off the main street, and we made our way slowly up a less busy side street. Two old women walked down the block toward us and I felt quite frightened of them. They both wore hats and scarves and seemed to be discussing me in low voices, leaning their heads together and gossiping about how crazy I was. I worried that they would push me, or arrest me, or mock me to my face. I decided the best course of action was to hide behind a trash can until they'd passed. I spotted one in front of a house and veered off, preparing to crouch, but Emmy straightened me back up and told me not to worry. "They're probably high too," she said, motioning to the old ladies. I stopped and looked at her for a long time. I wanted to let her know I could hear her, and I got the joke. I remember that. The rest is a jumble.

Emmy lives in London now, so I emailed her to ask her what happened after I tried to hide from the old women and she told me they were high too. Emmy responded, "You paused slightly, then said very slowly, *You were joking. I understand that was a joke.*" I had wanted desperately to tell Emmy that I was still there, just far away, and I recall needing to let her know I was still me, still funny. I attempted to tell her what was happening inside my head, but now I don't remember what I was saying, so I asked her. "You were very calm and very much narrating your experience, as though you were a writer doing research. It reminded me a bit of the documentary *Cave of Forgotten Dreams.* You were like Werner Herzog walking through the cave with a torch strapped to your head, making observations as you went."

As we walked, I felt more and more out of control. I know now that the THC was kicking in and I was getting higher and higher. My brain was disintegrating. I wanted to speak, but the words skittered just out of reach. Emmy told me that the last thing she heard me say was, "This will be a good forward story to tell people." I remain intrigued by my ability to come up with that novel way of saying that, in the future, our mutual friends would get a kick out of this situation. That means I knew it would end and I knew it would be funny.

We reached my apartment, and I immediately keeled over onto the bed. That's when my body really locked up. I could feel my hoop earring pressing into the side of my face. Emmy took my shoes off and looked around for what I'd eaten. Among my half-packed suitcases she found the box of candy, with just one piece left. She scanned the ingredients and spotted some small slips of paper printed with "25 mg." I hadn't seen them earlier. They indicated that there were 25 mg of THC, the principal psychoactive constituent of cannabis, in each piece of candy. I'd eaten three pieces, meaning I'd ingested 75 mg of THC.

According to a dosage chart created by Leafly, "the world's largest cannabis information resource," the recommended dosage for someone like me, a beginner with no tolerance built up, is somewhere between 1 mg and 2.5 mg of THC. Listed among people recommended for doses of anything over 50 mg of THC are "cancer patients" and "experienced users." It notes that a dose that high can cause side effects including pain, nausea, impaired coordination, and altered perception. So I was tripping, hence the bending railings and gigantic people. Large amounts of THC can also mess with neurological functions like memory formation and time perception, so that explains why I felt a fifteen-minute walk was days long, and perhaps why I forgot how to speak. The experience just felt so mysterious to me.

Months later, I look up the brand name of the edibles on Instagram. There are videos of gentle hands pouring chocolate and exquisite close-up shots of jellies. I direct-message them and ask to talk about the time I ate almost an entire box of candies and 75 mg of THC in one go. The man is nervous, since their business is not legal in New York State, so I agree to use Signal and no names. I explain what happened and he apologizes profusely. He is sweet and he says he is distraught, that he loves his work and believes when treated respectfully marijuana can be a wonderful help, and he believes in microdosing at 1.5 mg to 2 mg at a time. Somebody with no tolerance accidentally consuming a huge dose is exactly what he feared happening. I tell him it's okay, that I'm fine now and just wondering about a few things. I explain to him about how the physical world transformed and how my brain went to all the dark places, and how I felt like maybe I was going fully insane. "Oh, man," he says, with a rueful smile in his voice. "Maeve went for a ride." I tell him that I certainly did, and this seems like the perfect opening for my main question to him. "Where did I go?"

When I ask this, he laughs quite a lot at first, but then he does his best to answer. He explains that at a psychedelic-level dose, my notion of self probably changed. So there was a me with a narrative, the one walking home with Emmy trying to figure out what was happening, then there was the me as an observer, just watching myself. "Perhaps you widened the gap between your selves," he says. "It can be an interesting and pleasant experience to observe yourself. But your paranoia, that can feel a little like the sunken place. I guess that's the flip side of enlightenment."

There certainly was something otherworldly about my experience. I want to know about those eight hours I spent locked inside my head with all sorts of strange birds pecking and circling within. I want to know about consciousness and whether or not my mind is all I am, or where it begins and I end. Is that too much to ask some guy in a kitchen mixing weed with lychee fruit juice and vegan gelatin alternatives?

Back in the disheveled apartment, Emmy called a friend, an experienced weed user, and told him how much I'd taken, wondering if she should bring me to the ER. He told her I should be fine, and that I definitely didn't need to go to the hospital. Emmy sat beside me and told me gently, "You'll be fine. Mainly you'll just have to let it pass; maybe try to sleep." I enjoy some altered states: the otherworldly spaciness that comes with jet lag, the shoulder release after that first Negroni, even the glint of clarity after a cigarette. This state was not fun; it was something akin to drowning.

When I was ten, I hadn't seen the sea for a year because at that time my family lived in landlocked Zimbabwe. On school vacation, my parents drove us down across the continent to a beach in Durban, South Africa. I tried to swim, but it felt like I was being sucked under the water and out to sea. I screamed, swallowing seawater and snatching frantically at the retreating sand, which only ran through my fingers. I was caught in a riptide, a strong, narrow current that flows away from the beach. My mother ran in after me; she was steady enough to withstand the rip current. She yanked me out, and I was safe. She's always saving me, really, just not usually in such dramatic fashion. More often she notices me floundering before I do, and pulls me back in quietly.

I found out later that riptides do not suck people in. It feels like you're being sucked in, but no current does that. The struggle is what causes you to go under. I've thought about that in relation to my regular, unstoned mind too. I doubt my brain will change much, but I can at least learn to deal with it a little better. What if I stopped struggling against these great waves of anxiety and depression? I've tried various medications and done meditation retreats and changed what I eat and quit drinking and gone through different schools of therapy, but they stay coming. Now I was caught in the current of THC coursing through my system, and I didn't struggle. Eventually Emmy left. There wasn't anything she could do. She could hear me breathing, and every now and then I would murmur something unintelligible, but I had long since stopped responding to her questions. She knew she couldn't join me so she left me to journey on alone.

As I lay there tripping, I felt so terribly sad and guilty.

One of the stronger feelings I had in the swirl was a deep shame that this happened to me because of something I ate. Through my twenties I lurched secretly between overeating and frantically starving myself, so unhappy was I in my completely average body. One time I dieted and worked out so hard that my periods stopped for the best part of a year and another time I put on twenty pounds in one month. I became a shape-shifter.

I suspected the food was an addiction or an obsession that was covering for some greater lack, but digging into my psyche hasn't yielded any answers past bad luck and genetics. The starving and bingeing are gone now, but they've left me with a kind of disordered eating pattern, one that's easy to get away with in the hectic lifestyle I've adopted. I've used various tactics to get ahold of this: twelve-step programs, personal trainers, imagining Michael Fassbender is watching me when I eat so that I eat in a more normal way. Still, what is truly normal for me is to grab a slice of pizza and eat it on the way to the subway, or have pecans and carrots for breakfast and artisanal chocolate for lunch. Weeks later, when I told my sister about the accidental edibles, she said, "Maeve, what are you like? Some kind of puppy going around eating everything you find on the ground?" I laughed when she said it, but when I was high the shame tormented me.

I felt quite doomed that night, trapped now in a useless

body and vulnerable to all mental comers. My mind had free rein and chose to attack, mocking me for losing control of it, nananana-ing from the shore as I grasped at the sand that was logic. The plank in reason had broken because I wasn't strong enough to hold it steady.

Eight hours later I was able to sit up. My phone was still far too small to use, but eventually I was able to open my laptop. I got an email saying my flight was canceled because of a storm due the next morning. The airline offered an alternative, but I let it sail by, the words too fuzzy to deal with. I was so, so, so hungry, a truly bottomless-pit, teenager-after-a-game-of-football, nursing-mother hungry. I have no memory or clue about how I managed to order online and accept a food delivery in person, but I do have a flash of chomping into a beef burrito the size of a child's arm. It felt like that scene in *Jurassic Park* where the live cow gets lowered into the jungle by a crane and there's a frenzy of pulling and tearing as the dinosaurs gobble it up. All that's left is a dangling spine, or, in my case, two hands that smelled of meat and cumin.

In the morning, the Australian woman whose apartment I had been subletting returned to find me there, haplessly trying to pick up coins from the desk. Dexterity had returned to my fingers, but only just. It was our first time meeting, and I tried to be smiley and normal as I struggled with a troublesome pair of nickels, but she looked uncomfortable. She stood in the doorway with her large suitcases, and we both knew I was supposed to be gone. Subletting rules both official and unsaid make it clear that once the sublet is over, the person doing the subletting should certainly not be hunched quietly in the living room, half-packed bags strewn around, floor in need of vacuuming, fussing over small change.

I saw no alternative but to explain to her just what had happened. It felt like an event of great magnitude to me, but when I said it out loud, it shrank right down. "I accidentally ate a ton of edibles yesterday." It didn't even seem like a legitimate reason to be there, let alone be there staring at the bathroom and falling silent in midsentence because I saw my cosmetics and hair dryer and shower stuff, and the task of packing them all up felt epic in scale. "Sorry," I told her, "it's just that small tasks still feel big."

I'm impressed that I admitted that to another person. I was in a uniquely dire situation, sure, but in my regular day-to-day I could really do with that courage. Too often when my mental weather requires I take a raincheck, I either force myself to carry on or I retreat and cover it up with lies. The effort it takes to push through a business meeting at the same time as another layer of my mind is whirring with a hundred unbidden and terrible scenarios leaves me bone-tired, but I'd rather do it than cancel the meeting and admit defeat by anxiety. And "Oh, damn, I just got a deadline—I don't think I can make it to dinner" is much easier to tell a friend than "I feel like my skin is missing and I don't want you to see me like this."

The truth came out easily to the poor woman whose apartment I was meant to have vacated already. The high inevitably led to a deathly comedown. I stood next to her and looked into the kitchen cupboard and it was too much. My heart sank. *This will take hours to pack up*, I thought, uselessly gazing at the tea bags and tins of chicken stock. I had intended on putting everything back exactly as I'd found it when I moved in three months previously, but losing an entire day scuppered that plan. She was nice about it, but as I followed her eyes around the apartment, I saw her see all of the changes I'd made. Some of them would have been easy to fix, like moving the sofa and the desk around to face the window as she'd had them; leaving them be made it seem like I disagreed with all of her aesthetic choices. But I'd simply spent most of the past twenty-four hours paralyzed on the bed. "Oh," I heard her say from the kitchen, and then I heard the window open. The day I'd moved in, a statue of the Virgin Mary had caught my eye with her eyes and given me the heebie-jeebies, and I'd placed her gently on the fire escape and forgotten completely about her. In hindsight, that was rude of me. I watched silently as the Australian woman settled Mary back down on the desk I'd finally managed to clear, and Mary watched me with that sad smile of hers.

Because of my slowness to rebook my canceled flight, it was three more days before I could leave the city. I went to stay with friends, a family I used to babysit for. The kids are older now, and we mainly played cards and watched movies as the snow fell outside. I was very sleepy, day and night. Preteens are the perfect company when you don't have your wits about you. I didn't tell the kids what had happened, but they were delighted with the dopey way I couldn't follow the rules of the card games.

I finally got back to Ireland. I remember stepping into a hot shower. The water was hitting me, my mind felt clear, and I knew the THC had worked its way out of my system. I told people what had happened, having spun it into a funny story within a week, complete with the reliable beats of the long arms in Paper Source, the burrito, the coins. That's what it is, a goofy story about accidentally eating a load of edibles, but it also felt more elemental. I put the experience away. After a few months, I came back to New York, moved into a new apartment, and started a new job.

So why had that experience scared me so thoroughly? The fear I have that one day I will lose my mind is a whole can of brain worms I don't want to open.

At eighteen, that first time I saw a psychologist, I was relieved to tick off every box on the "depression checklist." I hoped I could hand it to her and not have to talk about how I felt. I still find it hard to, but at least now I know how creative I am, and what function that serves. Writing and making things help me to think and feel and process the world around me. Back then, rightly or wrongly, I was convinced that self-expression would be met with judgment. At home and in school—I would even say in Irish society at that time, the 1990s—the message was to behave yourself, to appreciate what you had, to get on with it. Despite its presence, there was no discussion of mental illness in my family until recently. I understand that completely and do not blame anyone.

When I got closer to thirty and gradually started to write, that too was cause for worry. The only other writers in our extended family were the most fragile or troublesome people. Addiction, mental illness, and creativity had melded together like some ugly metal sculpture in the otherwise pleasant public park of my family. My parents' valid questions about how stable a creative life could be, both professionally and financially, veiled the main concern I think they had. If I started digging around down there wouldn't I go too far, wouldn't I get lost?

I'm in a coffee shop in Brooklyn now, on my laptop. I honestly just ate avocado and feta cheese on toast. I'm a "type" in that I spend my days writing and thinking and talking about ideas, being serious and being funny and making a living that way. I can do ostensibly whatever I want. I laugh at myself, at how rarefied my world is now. This is the bubble people criticize, I suppose. I'm not upset about the bubble; I feel extraordinarily lucky to be in it. Don't those who are so busy criticizing the bubble understand the miracle of physics it takes simply to keep a bubble intact, the delicate combination of tension and stability necessary to sustain it? Every day I'm aware of how fragile bubbles are; bubbles float away, bubbles burst. I have this keen sense that if I'd been born at really any other time, I'd be in an asylum. Instead I found this place where my brain is valued. I get to meet writers and people who talk about ideas and read books and try to understand this moment.

Living as I do now, with a therapist and medication and an understanding that depression isn't a frightening monster waiting to tear my life to pieces, rather just a fact of life to be dealt with as well as I can manage, is a profound relief. Here, a friend can ask how I'm doing and I say "jittery" or "kind of sad," and that's fine. It's just that I thought I had a handle on my head. I believed by expressing myself the way I do now, creatively through writing, I was strengthening my sense of self. I didn't realize how scared I was of losing my mind until it started to happen, stupidly and all at once in a fancy paper shop at Easter. The day I ate those edibles I lost my mind, just for a little while. I fell down, through reason, and didn't know then what ground I would slam into, or even if there would be ground.

This story you're reading now is one I can sell as a funny story, one I've told with an easy fluency at dinner more than once, but it's taken me years to put it on the page. At times I had a twisted feeling in my stomach as I wrote it, other times hot tears jumped up into my eyes. Depression is extremely common, but I dearly wish I didn't have it. I wish that I could be fully immersed in a cliff walk or a new baby or even a good piece of cheese without my mind flashing to a place when the cliff is washed away and the baby is hurting and the cheese is some kind of weird punishment I've decided I deserve. Existential distress is painful and I hate it. As I write that I'm smiling because it's such a funny and impossible-to-solve problem that feels and is both real and unreal. I read what I can and research new treatments, like ketamine and psilocybin, and maybe something will come along to make me bright and shiny like I was as a child. In the meantime, hearing from others about their mental illness has been extremely helpful to me. Comics like Maria Bamford and Aparna Nancherla talk openly and often very funnily about the ups and downs their heads take them on. Just hearing other people speak about their setbacks is a relief. Better again, seeing them living their lives is the evidence I force myself to look at when living my own seems like an insurmountable challenge.

At least I got some better understanding of my psyche by horsing down a whole box of weed candy. For now, I am content with the candymaker's explanation, that I'd widened the gap between my selves. I figured some other things out too after tripping for hours. I understood that this terrifying time would be a "good forward story." I trust my mind more now after I thought it broke, because I know that even if it does break and I do fall, there are ways to climb back up again. I knew even then that I would write it down, however difficult that would be and however long it would take. I learned what I'd known before: that creating doesn't make you crazy, that it just might make you sane.

Good Acting

Collaborating never appealed to me. Perhaps it's because of the little Nazi boyfriend of the sixteen-year-old Von Trapp girl that I genuinely thought collaborating meant betraying someone, most likely myself. I translated this to my work and, while I admit that the stakes of a comedy career are not as high as a wartime betrayal that could end in murder, I tended to work on my ideas alone. I didn't collaborate because I didn't want to betray myself and my fledgling creative voice. If I let others in, surely they would blow the whistle like that little blond bastard did, and that would be the end of my fragile career. It's fitting that I can best explain this feeling through a film metaphor, because it was a film that made me understand how wrong I'd been.

One person—however talented or scared or both—cannot do everything alone. It's quite common to think otherwise, particularly about art. The isolated genius, the lone wolf: some brilliance can involve solitude, but to insist that one person can single-handedly create something usually involves erasing the work of others, or downplaying the lineage that came before. What it is instead is dominant egotism, or just some romantic nonsense, or perhaps even mental illness. There is something patrician and male there too—the whole "great man" trope that hulks at us from every corner of history and art. It's no wonder I felt I needed to guard myself and my creativity. Add to that the wild swings of self-esteem that swirl through the pattern of my life, threads that flip swiftly between *I'm the best* and *I'm the worst*. The truth is nowhere near as dramatic. I'm not a desolate wretch and I'm not a glittering prize. As it turns out I'm good at some things and not good at others, and that's fine because when I collaborate with a whole group of people who are good at some things and not good at others, we balance one another out. Collaborating isn't betrayal, it's a means to share and harmonize. In filmmaking, it's really the only way you can make a new world. This new world actually couldn't exist unless you join together all the things you're good at and not so good at with more or less equal parts of others, and trust that it will work out in the end.

Collaboration became truly essential when I was cast in a film. *Oh, cast in which part?* you ask, politely. *Oh, just in the lead role*, I reply, breathing heavily and close to your face. The fact that this happened is quite shocking to me. I had no experience of working on a feature, or even of acting on camera. (Off camera, watch me in conversation with a boring man I need a favor from and you will have to rub your eyes to understand that it's not Angela Lansbury in front of you, such is the quality of my acting.) I had some vague idea of what filmmaking entailed, but I had pieced it together from all variety of unreliable sources that I couldn't even name today.

I once asked my then seven-year-old nephew what he knew about America. He has a deep voice and a lisp, so please integrate that knowledge into his answer as you read it. "Well, Maeve, I know the children have them hats with cans of fizzies at the side and a straw coming into their mouth." "Fizzies" is our word for soda. I think my nephew got mixed up with those beer-can baseball caps men wear at ball games. They wear them kind of for fun and kind of because they're alcoholics and sports gives them permission to live that duality proudly. "That's all you know about America, that the children wear hats with fizzies on the side?" I asked him. And he said, "Yeah," and took a moment before adding, "And Wild Bill the cowboy; I think he was good?"

Unsure where to start, I walked away and left him to his Lego. He was hard at work building a rocket flown by a raptor.

My nephew's mixed-up and largely inaccurate image of America echoed my own ignorance of what filmmaking is like. It was something I'd heard of, and knew a little about from seeing it onscreen. And like America, the mythology built up around filmmaking almost obscures the grubbiness inherent in its creation. What if America is a bunch of diabetic kids with blackened teeth, too zonked out to learn? Then is filmmaking a grimy and bloated industry where only the sickest individuals make it to the top? I didn't have a clue about the truth then, and am not much further along after the whole process, but I know a little more now. I took the role and got down to the business of filmmaking, and quickly realized that collaboration was the key to the whole thing. I mean, what was Hitchcock without his birds? There are so many creatures and objects involved in any one film, it is impossible to credit one person and mortifying to accept that credit if and when it is assigned to you.

I was acting in a very silly and good horror-comedy film written and directed by two friends of mine. To get acting work, I have some very specific advice based on my own experience. I tell young actors to befriend the funniest oddballs they can, and if they ever ask you to be in their film, say yes and then wait. That's what I did. I met these two, Mike and Enda, when I was doing comedy in Ireland and they were in a band and making ads for TV. Both of them have big noses and low voices, so holding conversations with them at music festivals and crowded pubs was quite challenging. So I wouldn't say I knew them very well because I could never quite make out their words, but the vibe was always great. Many years later they wrote the script for the film, which is called *Extra Ordinary*, with me in mind. At that point I had basically gone it alone or worked on projects I could control tightly and claim as my own. I was tired of always relying on myself and I felt pulled toward, horror of horrors, other people! Although I didn't know where the pull would lead me, I felt it strongly in the direction of this film made by these two sweet mumblers.

The first time I walked onto the set I just saw a number of unshaven men in clothes that were either too small or too big for them, mainly combat pants with old gray T-shirts and black hoodies, draped in gaffer tape and electrical wires, clutching battery packs. I knew from watching film credits that there was someone called the best boy and another called the grip, and I wondered if some of these men were the best boys, the grips. I felt pretty shy and stupid and like I didn't belong there. I had decided when I turned thirty-five that reasonably half my life was over and I had gotten away with it thus far, so it was illogical to think I'd be caught now. (By "it" I meant existing largely the way I wanted to and not being forced to have babies or work as a manual laborer.) The dowdy men were muttering and shifting themselves and various objects around. I looked for the directors but couldn't see them. It turns out they don't actually stand behind the camera; the director of photography does that.

Like a sinister child, I silently watched the grown-ups do their jobs. This was Ireland, so nobody made any formal introductions, and it didn't seem right to march around introducing myself, so I kind of stood around in a dressing gown until one of the men emerged, wearing a puffy jacket, and said I could start the scene. I learned that the directors and assistant directors usually wear puffy jackets and drink a lot of coffee, and the younger crew members wear fleece jackets and smoke hand-rolled cigarettes. We had five weeks to shoot a ninety-minute film, which I learned was a short time for a lot of footage. One of the directors, Mike, said, "This feels like a race, like every morning we have to get up and do a race!" He looked really stressed, with flashing blue eyes, when he said that. But I immediately liked the idea, because we were all racing together.

On the second day I figured out that as an actor on a set, all you have to do is exactly what you're told. So, it's easy to just relax and take everything in while you're waiting to say your lines. Maybe good actors try to access something upsetting that happened to them once, or something cheering, or whatever the scene might be, but I don't know how to do that. And since it's only pretending, it's a better use of time to sit quietly and look around and try to figure out what the hell everyone else is doing. Something clicked as I watched the electrician consult with the first AD and the directors look over their storyboards with the DOP: I realized I was on a building site. My father has worked in construction all my life, starting as a surveyor and becoming a construction manager. It all made sense. Filmmaking is building.

The directors are the architects, dressed cool and having aspirations slightly above what's possible. They have storyboards, like architects' blueprints. The producers are the construction managers and estimators, keeping everything within budget, troubleshooting when the weather doesn't comply. The ADs shuttle between the directors and everyone else, just like supervisors on sites, with the first AD being the foreman. The sparkies and the chippies are themselves, and where did that leave me? As the makeup artist (construction worker) troweled foundation onto my face and the costume checker (another construction worker) hauled my cardigan into place, I realized exactly where it left me. I was a concrete block, a length of iron piling, a prop to be placed wherever the architects specified, as long as that placement stayed within health and safety guidelines. I would fit seamlessly into their vision and did not need to worry or even think! I just needed to be a perfect concrete block in the right costume with all my lines learned off. Someone would even tell me where to stand and when to eat lunch. I've never enjoyed a job so much.

The acting "work" of saying lines and pretending to be scared or happy and kiss and slap people—all of that was totally fun and easy. I was surprised at how I took to acting, because in the years preceding the film I had developed a severe allergy to it, particularly acting onstage. In fact, I had to stop going to see any theater, one-person shows, musicals, and even long-form stand-up comedy shows. It came on me gradually, the way a deadly virus starts as a light tickle on the back of your throat. At a perfectly fine play one evening, I found myself biting back a smile as an actor talked about the death of her imaginary mother. The play was a hit, the actor receiving universal praise from all quarters. And here she was, crying tears that were physically real, contorting her face as her nose ran and she let out some ungodly wails. A laugh rose in my throat, but I swallowed it back with such force I made a kind of retching sound. I looked at my friend, who'd paid $130 for our tickets, and mouthed, "I'm fine."

My friend Jo asked me to go and see a show with her, a one-woman show full of pith and vigor, and I shook my head sadly and told her no. I explained that I couldn't, that I might be sick, like that one time I was sleeping on an airplane and woke up with a sinking, or rather rising, feeling in my stomach. I had tried my best to stay very still, to will my physical reaction away, but I could not. I barfed all over myself and the seatback in front of me, terrifying the young woman beside me. A similarly inevitable physical reaction would surely happen if I entered a theater again. Jo didn't look convinced. "Are you sure you just *don't want to go*?" she asked. I insisted then that I did, I wanted to support the arts, doing so is a key part of my identity! It was just that I knew the actor would be acting, saying things she had said before, imitating emotions, and I could no longer pretend that I didn't know that it was all pretend.

Over time, it became impossible for me to suspend reality enough to enjoy any form of acting. Perhaps it was like when you eat half a dozen eggs every day for some deluded diet and then you suddenly become allergic to eggs and any product containing eggs. I had built up a high tolerance for acting and then tipped over to a complete intolerance of any and all things acting related, especially when it was supposed to be in any way sad or serious or moving.

It got to me, the belief that acting was a perfectly acceptable way of spending our time. Acting is pretending to be somebody else, pretending to have emotions, pretending to die, to have sex, to murder, to admit murder. As children we have make-believe games all the time, and those games help us to process our lives and feelings. Perhaps living as I do in this politically fraught era with global events creating personal and emotional repercussions on my own reality, I simply ran out of time and tolerance for anything outside of the real. Coupled with an innate anxiety that assures me all manner of terrible things will happen, I've been around for long enough to experience the actual world in which terrible things do happen, as well as every other type of thing. I grew up, and funny and serious and sad things happened to me, and there seemed to be no time to pretend anymore. Like the rest of us, I was too busy lurching through my own comedies and tragedies with as much grace as I could muster.

Stand-up comedy generally consists of a set of stories and jokes a comic thinks of, practices, and repeats, literally called "a set." My job for many years was doing sets, the same ten or twenty minutes a night, or a full hour of the same set at festival shows. Many of us have a few minutes set aside in longer sets to play around with new jokes and stories, but in general the whole point is to work up a stellar set that will do the same job night after night. In the early days I would repeat my set like a mechanical doll, while my mind wandered around the bar or the theater and I waited for my body to stop gesturing and talking.

I began to understand that it was not a good thing, to leave your body night after night, so when I moved to New York and started a new show with my friend Jon, I told him we were never allowed to repeat the same set. "Only new material," I bellowed at Jon, who is a shy man. I felt good, like a selfish princess ordering another great big dress for a party that Jon wasn't invited to. He found it exhausting and nerve-wracking, constantly coming up with new stuff, but I was pleased. It felt more authentic that way, even if it did lead us down some dead ends. In fact, the exhilaration of scrabbling out of those comedy cul-de-sacs made it more fun than ever, for me.

As the years ticked by, I was sad to lose access to the part of me that could get swept away in a performance. I went to a trilogy of plays when I was fifteen, the Leenane Trilogy. I was by myself and completely enchanted, curled up in a red velvet seat for more than six hours, rapt in the drama unfolding before me, crying and marveling at the skill on display. I don't think wild horses could drag me there today. And if they did I'd probably be quietly disappointed at how performatively they stamped their hooves and tossed their manes. *Not real!* I would think. *Playing a part!*

I found I couldn't bear to watch acting onscreen either. That's how I got stuck living exclusively in the world around me, without a stage or a screen to escape to. I was happy that way, for a while. There was plenty to occupy me every time I opened my eyes or asked a question. This life is so wild, so mysterious, it's impossible to get to the bottom of it: the man beside me on the train who told me he was a lawyer back in India but could never get promoted to a judge because he was Sikh, my little niece growing up so quickly and getting her ears pierced and telling me on the phone she was shaking like a leaf in a tornado, my friend I loved who did me dirty, the pace of it all and the fact that it will end and could end at any moment. Truly, you couldn't make it up.

When I knew the film was happening, I started to watch other films again. I watched films I had seen and loved as a child, and felt no embarrassment at all about the acting. When it came time for me to act, I was lucky to be surrounded by actual actors. I was also distracted by the newness of the entire process. This allowed me "not to think about it too much," which is, infuriatingly, the best way to do so many things, including being in a horror-comedy film. That is not to say that the whole thing was a breeze—some of the other parts of the job were hard. As I write this, I can see from my window three roofers doing their work on a freezing November afternoon, rushing to finish their day's work while the light holds. I can't honestly say that my job was more difficult than balancing on a ledge and cementing heavy slates onto felting, but permit me please to note the little annoyances I experienced on a film set.

When it comes down to it, unlike for roofers, there is a *lot* of interaction with other people. None of the cast are allowed to make their own way to the set, in case they trip over a wire or get lost, so a car and driver ferry the actors between their homes and the set. This inevitably meant being picked up early in the morning by a compulsively chatty Dublin man in his fifties, a former taxi driver who could make conversation out of thin air. His usual opener was to boast at length about how much caffeine he could handle. "Eight shots in this; look at that!" he'd say, holding up a Starbucks cup. I would think, *I can't see the number of shots*, but I would say, "Wow. That's actually amazing." Then the driver would remark on what every single other person on the road was doing, for example, "There's the fella in the blue Corolla now, making a left into that estate." I didn't mind the chatter, and he didn't mind when I asked him if I could learn my lines. "Do that, love," he told me. "I'm happy to chat away."

Sometimes as we drove the forty minutes to the set we wouldn't pass anyone, and that was when he would have to dive into the realm of the imagination. At least I hoped that was what he was doing when he pondered aloud the best places in the passing landscape to hide a dead body. "See inside in them trees there—say now a farmer was after killing his wife, just say anyway, he could pop her body inside of them trees and look, we'd be none the wiser." He seemed unsatisfied with my response, which was usually a murmur of agreement along the lines of "Oh, yeah." So he would press on. "Especially in winter, Jaysus, sure the cold alone would put people off looking for her." I'd be quiet then, and so would he, both of us lost in his creation of a world where the police and the missing woman's family and friends all calmly waited for the weather to pick up before they bothered to go outside and look for her.

As soon as I arrived on set, the costume ladies would show me what I needed to wear. It would be laid out in my trailer, earrings and socks alongside it on the table. They were glamorous middle-aged Irish ladies covered in scarves and swathes of fabric that vibed with the land and shore around us, moss green and peat brown and gorse yellow. Whenever I wandered away from the set to go to the restroom or stare at a field, I noticed ADs standing discreetly behind me and speaking into their lapels, saying quietly, "Number one bathroom break" or "Number one resting outside."

They held umbrellas over me when it drizzled and made sure I got my lunch right on time. It seemed like they just really cared about me, Maeve, and wanted me to be safe and content. I knew that on this building site, I was something essential, like lead in a roof or iron in a piling. If I somehow snapped or dulled, everyone else would have to begin again with a new piece. At first it was irksome, being followed around, all my movements being reported back to who knows how many others. But when I realized I wasn't really there as myself but as an element, a thing they needed for the bigger project, I didn't blame them for watching and tending me carefully. I tried hard to keep quiet and not have too many thoughts of my own. It was a relief, really.

Another relief, even more unexpected, was that I began to love invention and performance again. By devoting myself totally to creating a brand-new world where nothing bad really happened and everyone in it was guaranteed a happy ending, I suddenly understood why others did it. The outside world can be too much, it just can. Being silly and being creative and trusting other goofballs doesn't solve anything, but when it's possible to create a little escape hatch, isn't it cruel not to?

By the end of five weeks I adored all of the crew, having seen how talented they were and how hard they worked. Very quickly into filming I began to see all the small ways they were helping me, like making sure my head was supported when I was supposed to be getting dragged on the ground by a demon, or giving me a wink and a smile of support at one a.m. on a cold night when I knew I'd messed up and was responsible for keeping more than thirty people outside in the dark for longer than necessary. This experience has allowed me to enjoy films again, humming along on a dual track that appreciates the plot as well as knowing that the actor not in shot is probably a little bored by the actor on camera. I look at the colors and I think about the nervous apprentice electrician rewiring a light. When the scene drags I picture some flirty AD charming the prop assistant on a cigarette break. It's more fun to watch films that way, and soon I can even imagine myself going back to a theater to watch a play. Learning that the collective bests the individual has allowed me to enjoy art again, however silly it is, because without it, all we have is reality.

Misneach and
Rumors of War

Misneach

<small>FROM OLD IRISH *meisnech*,
MEANING "COURAGE, SPIRIT"</small>

This is a story about two statues. When I hear the word *misneach*, I can only picture a horse thrusting forward to battle, a teenage girl facing into the unknown with her gaze steady, an entire community betting on itself to smash old constructs and start over stronger. This image comes to me because that's what I saw the day I learned that word. *Misneach* is the title of the sculpture I just described, a teenage girl in a sweatsuit and sneakers riding a magnificently muscled horse, by the artist John Byrne. It stands twenty feet high on a concrete plinth outside Trinity

Comprehensive School in Ballymun, Dublin. When I hear *misneach*, it sends me hurtling back through time to 1916 and 1957 and 1921 and it sends me shooting across the world, to India and Kenya and America.

Misneach came to mind as I stood in Richmond, Virginia, in the pouring rain, gazing up at the second statue in this story, of another teenager on another horse. As the raindrops tapped a rhythm of change on my umbrella, I took in *Rumors of War* by the artist Kehinde Wiley, standing as it does on a huge stone pedestal. The horse is in its prime and in full flight, and there's a Black teenager with short dreadlocks and Nikes and a tracksuit on, holding the reins with one hand, facing off to the side, looking alert and sure and strong.

Rumors of War, unveiled outside the Virginia Museum of Fine Arts in December 2019, was inspired by the statue of Confederate Army general J. E. B. (James Ewell Brown) Stuart, a statue that stood on the city's "Monument Avenue" since 1907. I had seen that one the previous year, the first time I came to Richmond. I was there to record a comedy radio show, and it was on the drive in from the airport that I first saw the statues. I craned my neck in the taxi to see these half dozen gigantic stone men on horses, spaced evenly down an elegant grassy mall. All of them were huge figures in the Confederate war against the United States except for, incongruently, the Richmond-born tennis champion and civil rights campaigner Arthur Ashe, a 1990s addition and the only Black person represented. Ashe stands with a tennis racket and a book, surrounded by children. This represents his legacy as an athlete and his life's work of promoting education and is a head-shaking contrast to the other monuments, all of them looking considerably more battle ready. Then along came Wiley's Black teenager on a horse. He wasn't in conversation with these monuments, rather with the people who lived in the city they dominated.

Just six months after *Rumors of War* was unveiled in Richmond, a Minneapolis police officer named Derek Chauvin would kill a Black man named George Floyd, a crime that was witnessed on video by millions around the world. The news of Mr. Floyd's killing, one in a long line of Black people killed by police, brought with it immense pain, anger, and grief, and quickly set in motion the largest movement of protests this country has ever seen. In Richmond, as in cities and towns across the world, residents marched and raged and wept together. They gathered at the Confederate statues, these tributes to men who fought to keep Black Americans enslaved. This was not a new fight—petitions and pleas to remove the monuments had been going back and forth for years—but now it had a new urgency. Protestors spray-painted the obelisks and shone bright white lights stating

"Black Lives Matter" on the dark stone of the central General Lee monument, creating another image that shot around the world. This time it was not a Black man gasping for breath under the white knee of a state servant, it was a simple but still revolutionary statement. Arthur Ashe and *Rumors of War* stood untouched, but within six weeks of Mr. Floyd's murder, the city of Richmond removed J. E. B. Stuart and three other Confederate monuments, leaving empty plinths up and down Monument Avenue. The largest statue at the center of Monument Avenue is General Lee's, and the police and city officials quickly ceded the ground around him.

At the unveiling of *Rumors of War* in 2019, Wiley said this: "In these toxic times art can help us transform and give us a sense of purpose. This story begins with my seeing the Confederate monuments. What does it feel like if you are Black and walking beneath this? We come from a beautiful, fractured situation. Let's take these fractured pieces and put them back together." As well as the similar image of a teenager on horseback I saw in *Misneach*, it was this instinct and this intention that connected both monuments, the artists' decision to reimagine something terrible into something beautiful.

Putting the fractured pieces of history back together is exactly what *Misneach* does. John Byrne, the artist in that case, was inspired by another statue, one that had been blown to pieces by the Irish Republican Army, the IRA, in 1957. Perhaps when you hear "IRA" you think of the newer iterations of the IRA that sprang up from the 1970s on and fought mainly in the North of Ireland. They are largely known as "the Provisional IRA." In this case, I'm talking about the anti-imperialist IRA that bubbled along throughout the middle decades of the twentieth century. The "Old IRA" was the first legitimate army of the newly formed Irish Republic; after that came the civil war, and the IRA referred to is the force that did not agree with the peace treaty and continued to resist any British involvement in Ireland, as well as the new Irish government. I hope that is clear, because there is a test at the end of the chapter. So, back in 1957 the IRA was quite active in destroying monuments, and a frequent target of theirs was the statue of Field Marshal Gough, a British army officer who fought in nineteenth-century colonial wars in Europe and China before eventually serving as commander in chief in India; this is the statue *Misneach* was inspired by. Gough was born in Ireland, and his military career ended with the highest possible rank in the British army. The brass statue of Gough was erected on a towering plinth in the center of Dublin's Phoenix Park in 1880.

The metal that made Gough's statue was collected from five tons of "enemy cannon" in India and China, the material of a violent struggle by the people he was colonizing on behalf of the British army. Then, a century after that, it was blown up by a different group of anti-imperialists, this time in Ireland. When I learned that, I'm sorry to tell you this but there is no other adequate way for me to explain the extent of my awe: my mind, like the statue of the brutal old soldier, was blown to pieces. How could it be a mere coincidence that the very metal dug out of the ground, the minerals so craved by the rapidly industrializing Britain in the nineteenth century that the nation would maim and kill entire populations for access to them, could be used as a weapon against the colonizers but fail to stop their terrible work? And then for that metal to be brought by those same conquering savages across the ocean to another land they had presumed to take hold of, and molded into a triumphalist public statement over an already cowed people, seems a bit far-fetched. Next, in a twist nobody could have seen coming, except for those who know every empire must fall, that statement, in the form of a statue, was destroyed by people hungry for as complete a freedom as they could imagine. The metal lived on, just changed shape, eventually being reconstructed back into the statue again, which would then serve as a mold for *Misneach*. Doesn't that seem like a particularly potent substance? If you've ever stood alone in a prison or a house of worship or even a well-loved kitchen and somehow got a sense of the place, that is the walls talking to you. That is the wood and the stone and the cotton telling you a story. I think the metal of a monument has something to say too. According to Jane Bennett—the brilliant political theorist, not Lizzie's pretty sister in *Pride and Prejudice*—this is "vibrant matter." She argues, "Edibles, commodities, storms, and metals . . . act as quasi agents or forces with trajectories, potentialities and tendencies of their own," and in the case of the metal used to make Field Marshal Gough's statue that is quite stunning to consider. Gough was by many accounts barbaric in his behavior in the colonies. He was nicknamed "the Hammer of the Sikhs," which is quite repulsive when you consider that he was the aggressor and all of this conflict stemmed from the British Empire's belief that it was entitled to take and own any part of the world it wanted and to control all of the people there. Today, India and Ireland are far from the British colonies we once were. I wonder if the metal understood that too, or even helped us to figure that out.

In Ireland, the question of what to do with monuments to former oppressors was just one of many gigantic conundrums facing the brand-new Irish Free State upon its birth in 1921. It had been a difficult labor: after almost eight hundred years of British occupation the people suffered a short but brutal war of independence that ended in the foundation of the Irish state but also cemented in place a partition that would leave six counties in the north of the country part of Britain. That was followed by another war, shorter but arguably more brutal, this time a civil war waged over the partition and other attempts by Britain to retain a hold on Ireland. During and after the civil war, whole infrastructures had to be created and maintained. The names of towns and streets would be changed to reflect an independent country. My hometown was known as Queenstown until independence in 1921, when it was renamed Cobh.

In the cities, the landscape was punctuated by these towering statues and monuments. In the decades following independence, the monuments erected by the British all throughout Irish public space were removed by both the new Irish government and, as in Gough's case, a host of less official ways involving gelignite and other explosives. Monuments have long been handy targets for direct action. The most famous target in Ireland was probably Nelson's Pillar, a statue of Admiral Nelson standing over 130 feet tall on a pillar slap-bang in the middle of Dublin. It was placed there in 1809, less than a decade after yet another failed rebellion in the city, a mark and a warning to the population.

Nelson had never even visited Ireland; his monument was not a commemoration. It was a political act, as all public monuments are, a towering reminder to the Irish of who was in charge. The pillar was blown up in 1966, by whom it was never officially known, and its destruction didn't harm anyone and was widely celebrated. A song about it, by the folk band the Dubliners, shot to the top of the charts. It makes me laugh listening to it today, especially the live recordings where everyone is singing along, their voices gleeful as they tell of Lord Nelson's ascent into the atmosphere to become Ireland's own contribution to the global space race. It must have been so much fun to watch the Irish army blow up the jagged remains of the pillar, as five thousand people reportedly did, then rush in to get a small lump of the Wicklow granite and tuck it into your cardigan pocket before you headed to the pub for pints with your friends, just smoking cigarettes and eating toasted cheese-and-onion sandwiches in a snug, talking about socialism with other dark-eyed, curly-haired youngsters.

The IRA put enormous effort into destroying various symbols of British imperialism through the years, and it's generally accepted they are the ones who got Gough; in fact, they got him repeatedly. On Christmas Eve in 1944, somebody even managed to saw his head off. I have long associated the night before Christmas with a slightly wild feeling. Perhaps it's because we grew up believing the old pagan legend that animals can talk on Christmas Eve. Or perhaps it's because we grew up just down the hill from a small church that held midnight mass on Christmas Eve, and the pub that would serve parishioners after mass, so we would wake that night to the sounds of rowdy grown-ups stumbling home in the dark country night. In any case, it is thrilling to consider a group of people—for surely it wasn't just one or two—meeting on a freezing Christmas Eve night with a hacksaw. The head would surely have been a charming Christmas gift for any anti-imperialist, but they didn't keep it. The statue stood decapitated for months until the head showed up in the River Liffey, peeping out of the mud-flats at low tide.

Gough's head was soldered back on, and he remained largely intact until the 1957 explosive attack broke him into pieces. The remains of the plinth and the statue were quietly withdrawn from public view and put into storage, where they remained until the late 1980s, when a member of the Guinness family bought him from the Irish government, with strict instructions to remove him from the country. Sir Humphry Wakefield, a descendant of Gough's, eventually claimed him, had him restored, and settled him at his home in the north of England, Chillingham Castle. It was there that *Misneach*'s sculptor found him and was able to make a mold—not of Gough, just of the horse.

Misneach was commissioned as part of an art program for the Ballymun Regeneration: a remaking of an entire neighborhood, via a public and private partnership that cost hundreds of millions of euros and took more than a decade to complete. The renovation was almost completed, until The Great Recession happened in 2008. The recession meant that once again Dublin ran out of money, this time before it could place the statue in the center of Ballymun's business district as planned, because the business district wasn't completed. So they had to put the statue, one and a half times larger than life, somewhere else. The young woman who modeled for the girl on the horse, Toni Marie Shields, went to Trinity Comprehensive School, and it must have seemed fitting for the kids there to see themselves. That is the story of how *Misneach* came to stand outside the school building looking just like courage, looking just like the kids inside.

"Big Houses" were another symbolic target in the destruction of imperialism. These houses, which punctuated the landscape in rural Ireland, were where Anglo-Irish landlords (usually Protestant) lived—huge homes on large swaths of land gifted to them by the British government. Smallholders (usually Catholics) rented the land from them for farming. In America, plantation houses were lived in by the "planters," or farmers who owned land across the southern states of America and who enslaved people. There is not a comparison to be made between what enslaved people were subjected to and the experience of Irish smallholders. The thing I find interesting is what happened to these Big Houses on either side of the Atlantic. In the past in both places, the buildings were symbols of power and control. Over time, that changed, but it evolved very differently in Ireland from the US.

The owners of the Big Houses in Ireland were hugely powerful throughout the nineteenth and twentieth centuries, holding political office in the British administration and owning almost all of the land in the country. That was up until a series of policy changes were set in motion to transfer some ownership to the Irish themselves. This transfer was made because of pressure from the Irish, as a way to quell insurrections; the owners and residents of the Big Houses were compensated and they stayed on in their homes. So if their power had subsided since the land redistribution of the late nineteenth and early twentieth centuries—as well as the huge economic hit they took in the famines of the previous century, when their starving tenants could not keep paying them rent—why were so many Big Houses targeted by the IRA during both wars? Some were destroyed in reprisal for attacks by the opposing British army, others so they could not be used by those soldiers as billets. More Big Houses were burned in the civil war than the war of independence, and part of that is because the IRA understood that the houses were potent symbols dominating the geography of the countryside. Almost three hundred Big Houses were blown up or burned down between 1919 and 1923.

In most cases, nobody was hurt in these arson attacks; the families were forewarned, and in some cases the IRA men would help them to move out their belongings before dousing the places with petrol and setting them alight. In some horrific cases, though, the IRA did kill the people inside. The psychological impact of destroying these houses was significant. In his book about that time, IRA commander Ernie O'Malley wrote that he had his soldiers, known as "Volunteers," train on the grounds of Big Houses to "rid them of their inherent respect for the owners."

The Big House loomed large not just in the physical landscape but in the minds of the people it controlled. Using and abusing the physical Big House could only help to break the psychic spell dictating that one group of people were somehow superior to another. Black Americans never had the opportunity to do that with the plantation houses. When slavery was finally abolished, many formerly enslaved people became sharecroppers, tenant farmers who paid the landowner with a share of their crops. When I learned that, I understood how close that new arrangement was to Ireland's old arrangement with the British. Our baseline injustice was a vast improvement on their former status. The Big

Houses in America were not razed to the ground but continued to profit from the labor of formerly enslaved farmers. They were preserved. Some Big Houses on plantations are used to educate the public about what really went down there, but many more of them are used as cute places to have your wedding. Sometimes the stories you have been told need to be destroyed and rebuilt using materials closer to the truth.

That is what brought me to Richmond, where I walked the mile or so from *Rumors of War*, the Black teenager on horseback, to the Robert E. Lee monument, past the pedestals that until recently held Confederate monuments. The empty plinths made for a strange energy in the landscape of the city—it felt like the silence when you accidentally walk into another family's argument. And that is what the empty plinths represent, two sides in disagreement about what the past meant, not ready yet to give over to the future. Far from an intellectual exercise, the question of what to do with monuments and statues is as real as it gets. A process as brutal and racist as chattel slavery has never been seen before or since; it's not comparable to colonization, and nor is a straight comparison between Robert E. Lee and Field Marshal Gough possible. The resonance I feel between Ireland and the US is that of two places struggling to hold their history and their present moment together in a way that stops them from ripping completely apart. Living in the US, I've listened with rapt attention to the arguments for what to do with Confederate statues and the names of all manner of places, from army bases to streets to towns. Sometimes when I sense the roiling pain just under the surface here, I want to let Americans know they're not the first to feel this. Other communities and other nations have also faced this reckoning and this pain. There's not really a YouTube video that explains in under three minutes how best to critically appraise the history of a place through how it has treated its monuments, but it is useful to see what these other places have done. Ireland hasn't fully figured it out even after one hundred years of independence.

British oppression and imperialism are no longer a direct force on the life of a person in the Irish republic. Indirectly I think it does still linger, but the same cannot be said for the oppression meted out by white supremacy here in the US. That oppression and its material consequences are felt daily on Black and Brown people living here. Enslavement is long gone, but other white supremacist structures are on view as clear as a statue in a public park: poverty, redlining, and environmental violence are alive and kicking in many communities. Monuments are just one symbol of that violence, and the debate about what to do with them is painful and unpredictable. In Ireland in the 1920s, nobody knew the right answer either.

Not everybody in Ireland wanted British statues destroyed or removed. State papers show that the argument about the Gough statue continued up through the 1980s. Supporters argued that the country was in another deep recession and the capital city wasn't looking its best, and the statue was art, an object of beauty. Regardless of what it symbolized, wasn't it magnificent? *The Irish Times* reports, "It was one of the finest equestrian statues in Europe and at the time the only equestrian statue in Dublin."

The newspaper quotes architect Uinseann MacEoin's letter to the Office of Public Works; he was in favor of reinstating the statue because of its historical and artistic merit, despite his being from "a strong nationalist family." That was an understatement. As a young man Mr. MacEoin spent time in prison, interned for republican activities. In his later years, he wrote a number of books about the "Old IRA." His other work was to preserve and protect the buildings and the Georgian heritage of Dublin city.

In reading about his legacy, I found it fascinating that he fervently lobbied to repair and restore the Gough statue. Was he right? With hindsight, he was right about a lot. In the 1960s he fought furiously against developments like the Ballymun Towers, which he saw as segregation by class and possibly by religion, because working-class and poor Catholics were taken from the city and housed instead in the suburbs. His worst predictions certainly did come true in the case of Ballymun. People suffered greatly from being relegated to the tower blocks there without amenities or adequate public transport. He won his battle to get the statue of Gough reinstated in Phoenix Park. Through painful and difficult work by the community, the towers he never wanted are gone and Ballymun is safer and more livable today than it ever was. The statue of Gough is gone from Phoenix Park, but its progeny, *Misneach*, is there in Ballymun, as beautiful and proud as its forebearer but meaning something completely different.

On that rainy afternoon in Richmond, I left *Rumors of War* and made my way past the empty plinths to the one Confederate statue remaining on Monument Avenue, the Robert E. Lee monument. Charlottesville, Virginia, is an hour's drive from Richmond, and it too had a Lee statue that was ordered removed, back in 2017. That order catalyzed a group of Nazis and other white supremacists to call for the now notorious "Unite the Right" rally in August of that year. Counterprotestors showed up too, and one of the white supremacists, a man named James Alex Fields Jr., rammed the peaceful protestors with his car, killing a woman named Heather Heyer and injuring nineteen others. The Nazis were granted their wish, and the Lee statue in Charlottesville stood until finally being removed in July 2021.

The Lee statue in Richmond is an incredible sight. I

forgot about my damp feet and cold hands as I approached it, simultaneously strange and familiar as it was. The city put heavy concrete bollards around the traffic circle, and both the bollards and the plinth are completely covered in graffiti saying things like "Black Lives Matter," "Fuck the Police," and "Say Her Name." The statue is surrounded now by a ring of laminated tributes, around thirty of them, each one telling the story of a Black or a Brown person killed by the police, each one with a small bunch of flowers attached. A couple of raised beds in the community garden planted by activists had some late tomatoes growing, and people stood in small groups at the foot of the statue, taking photographs, reading the words, or just lost in thought. I spoke to some of them.

"It's hard to describe what I'm feeling, the hair stands up on the back of my neck. My skin, I have goose bumps, it's so powerful." That was Mary Kadera's response when I asked her how she was feeling as she stood looking up at the altered Lee monument. A white woman, she had lived all her life in Virginia. "To see this, it has been here for so long, and I never thought in my lifetime that I would see this kind of demonstration for racial justice. I didn't." She planned on returning later that day with her teenage son, who was playing at a golf tournament nearby. Generational connections became a theme of my visit: none of us just materialized, we can only exist through people who've lived in the past. Latisha Robinson and Dora Jackson, two Black women, stood at the other side of the statue, deep in discussion. "My mom desegregated schools. She wanted to see it," said Ms. Jackson, pointing to an older lady out at the perimeter. We talked about what was better, leaving the statue up or taking it down, and neither was sure of the answer. Ms. Robinson wondered if it was better to let it stand, to memorialize the brutality of racism. "Sometimes when you leave things standing, if you leave things open like this statue here, it's a reminder to other ethnicities, not just Black Americans—it's about anybody who has some systemic racism done to them—*this* is a representation of all of that." Ms. Jackson was not comfortable with Lee keeping his perch up high over the city, likening him to an overseer on a plantation. "I have six Black brothers. I pray for them every day, just for them driving on the street, just for them walking. It doesn't feel good, the fact that they could easily be down here partying or just walking, and Robert E. Lee is literally looking over Richmond. He does oversee Richmond."

I spoke to a couple named Elle and Jason, visiting Richmond for the weekend from Washington, DC, or, as they put it, "a city full of monuments to people who owned other people who looked like us." On my simplistic "should it stay or should it go?" line of questioning, Elle kind of laughed and said she wanted to burn it all down. But, she said, "I don't think we should remove all painful things from our memory. I do think that celebrating it is the problem I have with it; that is what is driving me to want it to just go away. Why should I have to see it every day? Like, just driving down the street? If I choose to go someplace that describes this terrible painful past, if it's in the history books as it should be, so that we learn from it, great." Then she took the opportunity to elucidate the peculiarly maddening experience of being Black in America in this moment. "But the irony is that a lot of the same people trying to keep these statues up are also trying to remove this history from our education system because they don't want *that*. They're trying to erase the word 'slavery,' trying to call us 'indentured servants' or whatever? No. That's not what it was. It was terrible, call it what it was." Many people on the right who are fighting to keep the Confederate monuments by arguing that to destroy them is to destroy history are simultaneously acting to, well, destroy history. Speaking at the National Archives Museum just weeks before my trip, President Trump said he would fight what he called an emerging narrative in schools that "America is a wicked and racist nation," by creating a new "1776 Commission" to help "restore patriotic education to our schools."

Jason liked the graffitied statue for this very reason. "This is at least demonstrating conflict in a way that it never has before, that's what I like about it. It's like, 'We don't all agree with this depiction of the story.' I like that juxtaposition very much. There was no other option. You won't let us have this conversation in our history books, you've turned it into an unnecessarily combative conversation in social life, it's like, wow, now I have nowhere else left to put this energy that *you* know I have every right to feel."

I point out one phrase, "Fuck Your Borders," and we talk about how that is a subset of the conversation about who gets to be in the country. Jason points out, "This monument is a relic of a conflict about who gets to be in this country. A couple of hundred years in, we still haven't had that conversation." Perhaps we're having it now.

The next day, I spoke to Amaya, one of the people behind the graffiti. She's my friend Chioke's ten-year-old daughter, and after a lunch of smoked lamb and salad we sat talking on the front porch of her house in Richmond. I asked her how she felt when she visited the monument. "The Lee dude, the guy on the horse? Another guy, ugh, I don't know these people's names. But yeah, I tagged him with spray paint. I got to write 'F12,' 'Fuck the Police,' and 'BLM,' for 'Black Lives Matter.'" As for her feelings, she liked the atmosphere there. "There were people walking around handing out water and Cheetos, so I feel like I come here, I get free food and I get to tag a Confederate statue? Like, this is all I need in life!" The fun she had that day, the giddy feeling of being able to safely and physically express something so often only felt inside, was surely shared by the little gang who showed up to wreck the Gough statue that Christmas Eve more than seventy years ago. Yet despite her joy at the graffiti on the Lee statue and the summer she had just spent in open conversation about how Black people are treated in America, Amaya was unconvinced of the long-term prospects for racial equality. "Overall, humanity hasn't really advanced. It's like, humans are still awful beings. I feel like if there are life forms on other planets, they should stay on their planet. Like, do not come to Earth. Really. Starting with politics all the way down to where we are now, it's . . . yeesh."

Amaya is right; it is . . . yeesh.

That evening I got an email from Elle, who I'd spoken to at the Lee monument. "I caught up with my mom about our visit. For context, she grew up picking cotton in the South and integrated her high school, so she's lived a life. . . . I think she's heartened by the reckoning we're seeing today. I mean, our people are from Mississippi and never would have thought that flag would stop waving!" In June 2020, Mississippi residents voted to change the state flag, which previously had a Confederate emblem, to one that has a magnolia in the center and the words "In God We Trust." The Black community had campaigned for decades to end the state's attachment to its Civil War era, and this was a huge success that stunned many. Elle continued, "Of course, it's been hard for her and others in my family to relive a lot of what they fought against then, but it seems she's also proud to see so many others take up that torch." Again, the generations were speaking to each other, and with great care and deliberation, and they were noting the changes and the progress that in some cases they set in motion themselves.

I truly hate the phrase "throwing the baby out with the bathwater," suggesting as it does a terrible moment of irresponsibility and a soaking-wet infant, naked and hurtling through space, but it's apt here. In a rush to undo past injustices and create a different future, what potentially gets lost? But what if it was a bad baby, an evil baby that did untold harm to the people it dominated, and what if the water was filthy and poisonous? Why not toss it out and never think of it again? That last part is not possible, though, as any of us who've been told to "just stop thinking about it" know only too well. Putting something out of sight doesn't automatically mean it's out of mind. Even as the head of Gough's statue was buried in the silt of a Dublin river, even as the horse's torso lay broken in a box for decades, the repercussions of his actions as a British army officer were felt every day. Direct consequences of British imperialism included the partition of India and Pakistan, resulting in pure horror and the deaths of hundreds of thousands of people there, and "the Troubles" in Northern Ireland, smaller in scale but with equally terrible repercussions for those involved.

Misneach is gorgeous; there's wit and truth to it, reflecting as it does the uncommon urban horse-riding culture of the young people in that community. Ballymun, the North Dublin city suburb it's located in, suffered for a long time from high unemployment, with poverty and crime rates above the national average too. In the 1960s, seven massive tower blocks were built as part of a social housing initiative. The buildings were named after seven of the leaders of the 1916 Easter Rising, Irish nationalists who were executed by the British in what would lay the foundation for the much bigger revolution just three years later. Unfortunately, these buildings proved disastrous for the people expected to live in them. As Dublin City Council explains online, "All went well at first, but soon they also discovered that they had nowhere to shop, the lifts kept breaking down, the heating could not be lowered and the promised public swimming pool, meeting places and play areas were never built because the government had run out of money." Conditions for residents worsened in the decades that followed, and in the year 2000 the government and the community collaborated on a complete overhaul, agreeing to demolish the towers and re-build homes, this time in a more humane manner.

Like Elle's mother and Chioke's daughter, and everyone who lived in the high-rises of Ballymun, all of us carry the past into the future. When I looked at where the original statue of Gough ended up, I found it was at Chillingham Castle in Northumberland, England, the home of a descendant of his, Sir Humphry Wakefield. Lady Wakefield is descended from the Grey family, one of whom was a British prime minister and at least one of whom made their vast family fortune through the Atlantic slave trade. On the Chillingham Castle website, Lady Wakefield's father is described as "a one-time Governor of the former Rhodesia, of the South African protectorates and, finally, of the then Mau-Mau stricken Kenya." I laughed out loud at the word "stricken"—the Mau Mau were simply an armed response to the British people who had stolen Kenyan land and abused Kenyan people. Kenya was "stricken" by men like Lady Wakefield's father, not by the Mau Mau, not by its own people waging war on the colonists. But it is clear from the telling that the Wakefield family still see the oppressed fighting for independence as some kind of aberration on the natural order of things.

The Wakefields' daughter, Mary, is married to Dominic Cummings, who headed up Britain's "Vote Leave" campaign resulting in Brexit and ultimately served as British prime minister Boris Johnson's chief adviser. Through carelessness or malice, nothing threatens the hard-won peace in Northern Ireland like Brexit does, bringing up as it does the question of borders and parity. Mary Wakefield and Dominic Cummings became quite notorious after driving over two hundred miles to visit their family during the first COVID-19 lockdown in March 2020. The trip coincided with Wakefield's birthday, but they insisted that all they were doing was getting childcare while Cummings recovered from the virus. In August 2020, the medical journal *The Lancet* published a study on the degree to which such events as these had undermined essential public health messaging, which was huge, and named it "the Cummings effect."

I don't know the best thing to do with Richmond's Lee statue, and can you imagine me showing up at a Richmond City Council meeting and pretending that I do? Me, voicing my opinions, having spent hours practicing my Southern drawl. What I do know, as previously mentioned, is that my hometown of Cobh used to be called Queenstown. It was named Queenstown because in 1889 it was where the British queen Victoria alighted from her ship to visit County Cork, and it was changed to Cobh when Ireland became a republic in 1921. I always thought "Cobh" was the Irish, or Gaelic, for Cove. It is pronounced the same way, and Cove was the island's name before the queen visited and it was changed to Queenstown in her honor. However, there is no such word as "Cobh" in the Irish language. It seems that in the nationalistic fervor of the moment the powers that be decided to get rid of any reference to the British queen and go with something that sounded kind of Irish, and that is how the island became known as Cobh.

During Queen Victoria's trip to Cork, in a true nineteenth-century caper, the city erected a statue of her on a parapet of Queen's College Cork, somehow timing their final hoist to occur just as she passed by in her carriage. The statue symbolized British dominance, a British ruler looking out over the city on the only site of third-level higher education in the city at that time. It was not until 1934, over a decade after the war of independence, when many students at the university wanted her statue removed, that the university authorities did so themselves, putting her into storage. They replaced her on the parapet with a statue of the city's patron saint, St. Finbar. Then, for some weird reason, they buried her in the college grounds, swearing the few staff who knew of it to secrecy. It wasn't until 1995, to mark the 150th anniversary of the university's foundation, that they resurrected her again. She would never again loom over the city, just as her descendants would never again rule over the country. But she was no longer buried like a shameful family secret.

Rather she was placed in a glass case as part of a history exhibit. When her great-great-granddaughter Queen Elizabeth II came to visit Ireland in 2011, she came to the school (since renamed University College Cork), took a peek at the Queen Victoria monument, harmless in its museum-like environment, and toddled safely home.

Life goes around in circles, it does, but sometimes those circles spin so hard they transfer something new to the next round. I want to hold America's face when it lights up with a fever I'm afraid will set her whole self aflame, and tell her that there's not an easy answer except to fight and to win and to get free, in all the ways that a person can be free. It's possible, I think, to demand that from yourself and from others. It takes *misneach* to get there, and I see that in Black Americans and those who fight with them, that particular kind of courage: a heart-based courage, a hopeful courage, a spirited courage.

Situational Awareness

I remember the Alamo, of course I do. I remember the evening I stood on the grounds beside the biggest bowl of queso I'd ever seen while a man, his face reddened with emotion and alcohol, stood on a makeshift stage and auctioned off a homemade gun. That was the president of the Border Patrol Foundation, waving his weapon gently overhead as those in the crowd nodded their heads slightly to make their bids known, and the sun dipped low behind the old chapel. My heart quickened at the sight of the rifle, as it does every time I see a gun. I was in San Antonio, Texas, for the 2020 Border Security Expo, to better understand where the border was headed, and this was the social event of the weekend. I had been to the Mexican border before, and spoken to and written about immigrants who live there or who'd crossed it at some stage in their lives. It was easy to find migrants to talk to about the border, and even easier to understand why they need to cross it. It was more difficult to understand and get access to the powerful forces that built and enforced this border. When I heard that there would be a whole convention center full of every player in the deadly game of exclusion and enforcement, milling around a selection of border paraphernalia for sale, I just had to be there!

I was nervous about the trip. Given I'm a naturally conflict-averse person about to spend three days with a large group of people ideologically opposed to myself, it would be fair to assume that the potential conflict was the cause of my jitters. But I was delighted by the opportunity to understand Border Patrol. I was nervous because the expo began on March 11, and the coronavirus's inexorable march was already underway. The United States did not yet understand the threat and was weeks away from lockdown. On March 9 President Trump stated the flu was more deadly than coronavirus and that nothing was shut down. "Think about that!" he tweeted.

I am thinking about that now, as I write this just fourteen months later with six hundred and forty two thousand people in America already dead, killed by the coronavirus.

Back in early March 2020, New Yorkers were still going about their regular daily lives. I had wavered. *Should I get on an airplane? Should I go to a conference with hundreds of other people in an enclosed space?* I hoped my decision would be made for me and waited for the cancellation announcement, but it never came. So I flew to Texas and found myself squeezing through dozens of suited men with buzz cuts clapping each other on the back. And now, on the second night of the expo, here I was trying to stand extremely still, worried any accidental movement might be interpreted as my bidding on a homemade rifle at the Alamo.

In all my years of living in the US, guns are something I've not been able to get used to. Every time I see a police officer my eyes are drawn to their gun, and I feel a trill in my chest. Aside from their primary function as killing instruments, I suppose that's their main purpose: to instill fear. At the 2020 Border Security Expo in San Antonio, I saw all kinds of guns, from machine guns and battle rifles lined up for sale to the personalized pistols sitting snug on the hips of the Texas Rangers guarding the entrance just outside. The Rangers patrolled the perimeter of the Alamo every night, not just this one, the "5th Annual Night at the Alamo" held "to pay tribute to Border Patrol Agents who have gone above and beyond the call of duty." The tequila flowed. Another gun sold. A small girl took the mic and sang "The Star-Spangled

Banner" in a huge voice, the crowd roaring lustily when she finished, some wiping away tears.

The little girl was Lauren Dominguez, daughter of a Border Patrol agent who was killed on July 19, 2012. Her father, James R. Dominguez, died after he was hit by a passing vehicle on a highway near Cline, Texas. Seven out of ten Border Patrol officer deaths are caused by accidents such as car collisions, falls from boats, slips down cliffs, helicopter crashes, heat stroke, heart attacks. Other officers have been killed deliberately by people they're trying to apprehend. Since March 1, 2003, when the current iteration of the country's border security agency, US Customs and Border Protection (CBP), came into being, forty-eight Border Patrol agents have lost their lives.

As you'd expect at an event honoring lost comrades, there was much emphasis on the valor and the sacrifice it took to work in such a job. They were mourning their own, and I felt a heavy sadness learning of these workers who had been killed while on and off duty. Later, I was amazed to learn that being a Border Patrol agent is not even close to the top twenty-five most dangerous jobs in America. You're far more likely to be killed logging or collecting trash. I also learned, from reading an extensive investigation for *Politico*, that Border Patrol has been one of the nation's deadliest law enforcement agencies over the same period, shooting at least forty-six people dead since 2004.

In the same years, the number of people who have died in CBP custody is far higher. In 2019 alone at least fifteen people, including children, died in detention after seeking asylum from CBP. Migrants and sometimes citizens have also been killed outside of detention centers, shot by Border Patrol agents, driven off the road and killed in car wrecks, or have died from dehydration in the desert where Border Patrol agents slashed water bottles left out for them. Many thousands of migrants have also been rescued from the desert and the rivers by Border Patrol. In truth I don't know how many deaths the Border Patrol is directly responsible for, or which deaths it could be morally culpable for, considering for the most part it is simply enforcing policies created by our own representatives in government. Besides, I had not come to San Antonio to play morbid number games in my own head.

I was there to look for answers to questions that have dogged me now for a decade, since I became an immigrant myself. It didn't take me long to figure out how much easier my path to America was compared to the one that literally most people in the world would face. I'm white and young and European, working in an industry that is catered to by the US immigration system. I met other immigrants with very different stories of very different welcomes, and I made a podcast and wrote about the general experience of trying to get into the fortress that is the US. The counterintuitive part, for me at least, is that while America is the only destination available to so many seeking asylum, my case couldn't be more different. I'm free to move around the world, but America was happy to accept me almost *because I didn't need to be here*. Meanwhile, people die trying to get here and those of us inside the borders barely give it a passing thought. If there is a concern about migrants, it's not about their humanity or their welfare, it's about what they might take from us, despite all of the evidence and the history that point in the direction of America needing migrants.

I'm not objective, just as CBP is not, just as nobody is. I hope that having a point of view does not mean I cannot be fair. My point of view is evolving but fundamentally this: migration is a human right. "Open borders" is consistently used by right-wing Americans as a frightening threat, one that only a lunatic progressive would even consider. I feel relatively calm about it, though, and look forward to exploring how it could be possible and what kind of a future it could provide. I am more interested in interrogating the *opposite* of open borders, because that is our lived reality.

Borders and nation-states, along with all of the laws and the violence that hold them together and apart, are relatively new compared to the timeline of humanity. I used to take them for granted, figuring that of course a country has borders, how could it be otherwise?

My former position now seems poorly thought through, if not willfully ignorant. It makes little sense to me, a person born on an island divided by a chaotic border that caused a bloody war, to uncritically take borders to be something as natural as geology. Ireland was divided in two following the Irish war of independence in 1921, leaving six counties in the north as part of Britain and making the rest a republic. To this day, that partition has deep scars that threaten to tear open and bleed again. Borders are man-made, with all the inherent flaws that inevitably entails. Even calling borders "man-made" is obscuring the fact that many of the world's borders were made by a specific group of self-serving and racist men. The Middle East was divided ludicrously, with straight lines, by a British and a French man in 1916. Thirteen European nations parceled Africa into fifty crudely cut up "countries" back in 1884, disgracefully jamming over one thousand regions and cultures into them and leaving the continent vulnerable to every kind of pain imaginable in the century to come.

The southern border here in the US, the two-thousand-mile line separating this nation from Mexico, is the one I was struggling to comprehend in San Antonio. The Night at the Alamo was held in conjunction with the Border Security Expo, a two-day event that "offers federal, state, local, and international law enforcement from across the country and around the globe the education, solutions, and connections to make critical decisions needed to provide border security from every kind of threat imaginable." Basically, it was a CBP conference and an industry and weapons fair under one hugely high roof at the Henry B. Gonzalez Convention Center, in a year that saw CBP receive its biggest budget to date. Border Patrol is the CBP's federal law enforcement arm within the Department of Homeland Security (DHS). I wanted to understand Border Patrol, to explore what motivates it, and to see what its parent agency, CBP, planned to do with its $15 billion budget.

Despite the looming pandemic, my flight to San Antonio was full, and when I landed I couldn't find a taxi, so I ordered a Lyft. The driver told me it was his first week driving for Lyft, and I told him it was my first time in San Antonio and we agreed it would probably take longer than necessary to get to my hotel. He turned out to be a Kurdish journalist who had claimed asylum in the US after having filmed some atrocities committed by Saddam Hussein. He'd raised three daughters in Texas, and each one was a medical professional. I asked him if he felt that the risks he'd taken in his life had been worth it, first, in being a journalist under the Hussein regime and second, in fleeing to the US. On the first point he said he had no regrets, and he believes to this day in the power of journalism to expose the truth. In fact, he was considering taking media classes now that his last child was through college, though he laughed a little at the idea in the telling. On the question of leaving, it seemed to him he had little choice. He said something I've heard again and again from every kind of migrant, that his own life had been ruptured, and never recovered its past quality, but that his children benefited in ways that he was seeing only now, sixteen years later.

I had secured a room in an old, worn-out hotel, with saloon doors and a kind of faded glamour I quite enjoyed, at least until I felt how grimy and thin the carpet was under my bare feet. I put socks on with my nightdress and opened the window onto an alleyway. The night air was clean and cool, but I was awoken by screams in the dark. A very drunk man was swaying up the alleyway screeching, "We WON, you motherFUCKERS." It was just after four a.m., and I couldn't get back to sleep afterward. What could he possibly have won? I wondered.

Later that morning, I walked to the conference center

and checked in beneath a huge banner urging "ALL DOMAIN SITUATIONAL AWARENESS." That phrase "situational awareness" was repeated again and again throughout the event, a motif suggesting that threats could be anywhere and everywhere. I sanitized my hands and found a seat in the back, with a space on either side, as the chief of Border Patrol, Rodney Scott, spoke about the past year's victories and defeats. He mentioned a consistent problem for Border Patrol: hiring. It's difficult to convince people to take this job, seen as dangerous, in remote areas. The immigration scholar Mae Ngai has written about the formation of Border Patrol in 1924, when Congress first approved funding for the agency following the Immigration Acts of 1921 and 1924. Those acts imposed numerical limitations on migrants, and the US Border Patrol was officially established for the purpose of securing the borders between inspection stations and preventing people from entering "illegally."

Ngai writes that the earliest ranks were made up of "former cowboys, skilled workers and small ranchers"—many had military experience, and "not a few were associated with the Ku Klux Klan." They did not have uniforms until 1928, and "a lack of professionalism plagued the force." Recent reporting on PBS found that among CBP's most successful recruiting partners is the Professional Bull Riders (PBR) organization, which recently renewed its contract with the government to promote US Border Patrol to its fans. "We have an exceptional base for them to recruit from," said Sean Gleason, the organization's CEO. "It's a lot about values . . . cowboy values." These values were not defined, but I take them to mean a kind of independent-spiritedness, a Wild West attitude. But do those Lone Ranger values work in an armed force that has grown increasingly powerful in the past twenty years?

After a huge, sustained influx of money following the 9/11 attacks, Border Patrol more than doubled in size from 9,200 agents in 2001 to 21,000 during President Obama's first term. Speaking to *Politico*, Richard Skinner, the DHS inspector general at that time, recalled, "If President Bush asked for 100 agents, Congress would add 200. You have to remember how scared everyone was. The mentality was we need more boots on the ground." This reference to "boots on the ground" is one you'll hear often when it comes to the Border Patrol. President Obama used it too, in a 2013 speech about immigration: "We put more boots on the ground on the southern border than at any time in our history." That's a military phrase, which might make you forget that Border Patrol is not a military organization. The merchandise for sale at the expo was sometimes branded as "battle ready" and "war ready."

While some CBP agents have a background in military

service, many people at the expo were now high-level CBP officials or people from industries that sell to them. Often these roles are interchangeable, with the same men moving from private industry to public service and back again. Jayson Ahern is one example—he's been CBP's acting commissioner and is now a principal at the Chertoff Group, a global security company. I say "men" because they really are almost all men, a fact I noted when I went to use the restroom and walked by a line of men waiting to use theirs. The last time I noted such a gender disparity was when I went to a reading in a bookshop, but the line then was all women. I imagined mentioning that to the men standing there patiently: "You see, it was my girlfriend's YA novel, about unrequited love!" Only 5 percent of Border Patrol agents are female, historically the lowest percentage of any federal law enforcement agency.

The point of borders is to keep people out, but the people inside the US, myself included, are quite literally heavily invested in this border with Mexico. It costs taxpayers so much money, billions a year, and we pay it almost without question. The following year would see public discussions about defunding the police, but I have yet to hear a sustained and serious discussion about our incredibly militarized border security industry. I do not blame any American who does not know about the massive financial commitment the country has at the border, but now I knew. I saw it with my own eyes, so what would I do about it? Nobody was holding me hostage in this country; I chose to be here. When I chose to move here, I believed I was choosing freedom, opportunity, and ambition. For me, that's largely the truth of how my American life played out, but it's not the whole truth. How free am I when others aren't free at all? What costs do those opportunities create, for me and for other people? How worthwhile is my ambition when it reflects values that are not at all mine?

I distracted myself from the snack table by idling past the items at the silent auction. The auction was held to raise funds for the Border Patrol Foundation that night at the Alamo and included a large framed portrait of Justice Brett Kavanaugh and his family during his swearing-in ceremony, with text quoting him during his hearing: "I like beer. Sometimes I had too many beers. I liked beer and I still like beer." If only I'd not spent all my money on the homemade rifle!

The pressure to grow CBP in the post-9/11 era resulted in lower standards for new hires. Increasing corruption has been the result. Border Patrol accidentally hired members of cartels, and agents were regularly caught smuggling both drugs and people. The entire CBP saw 2,170 arrests for misconduct—such as domestic violence or DUIs—from 2005 to 2012. That is nearly one CBP officer or agent arrested for misconduct every day for seven years. There was violence too: Border Patrol was singled out for an internal investigation following many years of excessive-force complaints. Not much came of it. One of the senior CBP internal affairs investigators, the now retired James Wong, told *Politico*, "Not a single Border Patrol agent for the last eight years has been disciplined for excessive use of force. With a workforce that large, that's amazing." Wong went on to say, "You go pull the stats on any medium-size municipal police force, pull the stats on the NYPD. At any given time, they'll have all sorts of excessive force investigations."

In March 2016 the National Border Patrol Council, the official organization representing 16,500 Border Patrol agents, endorsed the then presidential candidate Donald Trump. The first week he took office in January 2017, President Trump signed an executive order for five thousand new Border Patrol agents, along with more border wall between Mexico and the US. Back in Texas, I listened as Chief Scott lamented onstage that the Border Patrol can't recruit directly at universities because of potential protests that he feared might overrun local police departments.

Protestors play what I suspect is an outsized role in the mind of Border Patrol. During the event at the Alamo, the emcee, a former Fox News host named Bill McCuddy, referred to the protestors outside, a peaceful bunch of about thirty people holding up signs, ringed by police and Texas

Rangers. During the auction their chants floated in on the breeze, and he quipped, "Is that one of the protestors making a bid? Who would protest outside a room where everyone is packing?" to some laughter. He followed up quickly with, "Excuse me; they have every right to do that."

On my way into the Alamo event I had peeked out from beneath my pink cowgirl hat and recognized some of the protestors from earlier that day. They made up a group of around twenty people, walking round in a circle on the sidewalk outside. There was an elderly Indigenous man wearing a sign saying "We did not cross the border, the border crossed us," and he did not seem threatening to me. Younger people held banners saying "Stop Racist Laws" and shouted "Chinga la Migra" (Spanish for "Fuck Border Patrol") at the uniformed officers who walked past, and held their middle fingers up as a couple of suited men recorded them on their phones. It was hot out, even at five p.m. "Well done, you guys!" I said as I walked by. They looked confused, perhaps because I was wearing a blazer and a lanyard at the time, but I meant it. I had a stabbing feeling of sadness, struck by how puny this show of resistance was against the might inside.

The exhibit hall of the Henry B. Gonzalez Convention Center is over five hundred thousand square feet, and within it stood hundreds of stands selling thousands of products designed to stop people in their tracks. Drones, cameras, firearms, walls, vehicles, sensors, cameras, dog kennels—everything was on show, everything was for sale. There were large IT security companies like Unisys and smaller start-ups like Dedrone alongside household names like AT&T ("Our first name has always been American") and Reebok ("tactical footwear").

It is certainly the case that powerful drug cartels have operated along the border for many years, and drug seizures by Border Patrol were up in 2018, but the business that most concerned Border Patrol at this conference was what they termed "people smuggling." A transnational criminal organization is a vague term, one which I understood to mean the network of people across South America and Mexico who charge migrants money in exchange for a range of services. That could be ferrying them across a river in Honduras, driving them right into the inland US, or paying the right Mexican cartel member to let the migrants pass safely. I wanted to know how the Border Patrol is tackling these much-touted "transnational criminal organizations," or TCOs.

Manuel Padilla Jr. said this: "There are upticks in Caribbean nationals and even certain African nations that are not unlike the Central Americans who continue to be lured by a very widening net cast by these criminals in the same way they profit from other illegal endeavors." The narrative was firmly on these ill-defined but supposedly multifaceted TCOs that Border Patrol speaks about as all-powerful, despite its own opposing and ever-increasing power in the form of money and men. I do not believe it's logical to blame a TCO regarding, for example, a Cameroonian migrant's decision to move to the US. It is also unclear how CBP is actually tackling TCOs; indeed, it seems far more invested in rounding up migrants and further endangering them in detention, or sending them back to Mexico without any due process for their asylum cases. I was left feeling that the insistence on looking only at the method by which some migrants make their way to the border, with no attempt to understand those migrants as individuals with agency, and individuals within larger systems, is purposefully obtuse.

I'd like to understand what Border Patrol believes constitutes effective policing of the borders. Despite extraordinary new measures aimed at deterring migrants, including separating families, limiting entries at official ports, and turning some people back to wait in Mexico throughout their immigration cases, 2019 saw an uptick in people crossing the border without authorization. Where there were once mainly single men crossing from Mexico, now there were families and unaccompanied minors from El Salvador,

Guatemala, and Honduras, as well as Cameroonians, Cubans, and even Syrians who had made the arduous journey up through Mexico to get to the border. The combination of inhumane US policy and increasing push factors from sending countries resulted in chaos at the border, and an ill-suited Border Patrol tasked with humanitarian work.

I first heard about the Border Security Expo from Marianne Madoré, a sociology researcher and one of the authors of an ethnographic study of the 2019 Border Security Expo. That year, with more families and children than ever arriving at the border, and the separation of families and deaths of children in CBP custody making headlines and causing outrage among the public, Border Patrol was on its heels, struggling with this new reality. Its representatives spoke on panels about rescuing migrants and providing diapers and baby formula.

The only time I eat in bed is when I'm in hotels. It feels like a treat that way, whereas if I started doing it at home it would feel like a defeat. That night I tucked under the sheets with all the pillows propping me up like a Victorian invalid, one who is somehow strong enough to eat beef jerky and read that paper again. Do you ever have a moment when you find yourself surprised at how content you are? Those moments tickle me because they are so unpredictable; I try to note them when they happen because when I string them together they really do lead me to a far more honest version of myself than my conscious mind will allow. I noticed how perfectly comfortable I was, alone in a lumpy bed in a Texas hotel eating shreds of dried beef and reading an academic paper. The researchers' conclusions were fascinating to me: "First, a humanitarian framework enables DHS (Department of Homeland Security) to elide responsibility in their direct role in pushing migrants to their death through PTD (prevention through deterrence) by arguing their need to intervene to save migrants from their own ill-informed decision to cross the border." The work helped me to understand a little more about some of the strange contradictions I'd witnessed that day. Border Patrol agents were feared and hated by many migrants. They were also often the first people migrants needing asylum had to find and make their claim to. They could snatch your child away forever, or they could quench your thirst and lead you to the promised land, the USA. The organization was plagued by corruption, but here in San Antonio at this conference the personnel were held up as heroes, the thin green line between innocent American citizens and the monstrous transnational criminal gangs gnawing at the borders.

There are countless facts being ignored by the US when it comes to so-called illegal immigration. San Antonio was once part of Mexico but was wrested away by violence and the colonial mindset of the burgeoning United States. The only reason a person becomes "illegal" is by another person making a law saying so, and over the years a variety of people have made a variety of laws going back and forth between the two states, proving that that illegality is produced, usually in a way that suits capitalism very well. Again and again, when the US needs workers, it finds a way to get them from Mexico.

There's the inescapable fact that most migrants at the southern border are Brown and Black, not white, and they are attempting to access a country founded on white supremacist activities like enslavement and genocide. Or the fact that building a wall in one crossing area will only push people into another crossing area where they are more likely to die, and the fact that we are all just here in human bodies vulnerable to the sun and the heat.

I couldn't sleep, despite knowing I was not about to solve any of that by lying awake in the dark. Those nighttime thoughts burned off with the mist along the San Antonio River the next morning as I walked over the bridge to the second day of the conference. During a plenary panel about biometrics, I checked the news on my phone and saw that the death toll from coronavirus in Italy was rising. I drank coffee and fretted about who else might have touched the cup. Sitting and listening, I tried hard to keep the finely spun web connecting policies to realities, almost invisible at the best of times, from vanishing. The speakers discussed "expediting the workflow, opening the aperture on how funding decisions are made and how the private sector can partner with the operator in shaping efforts to improve biometrics for all." I continued to zone out. Then one of the panelists mentioned "juvenile alien fingerprints" and how these fingerprints were not ideal for identification purposes. "DNA testing would be preferable," he said, in case the adult traveling with the juvenile was not in fact related to them. I was back in the room, riveted.

Here was a man calling real-life babies and children "juvenile aliens." You know, the juvenile aliens with burgeoning personalities and adoring granddads and vulnerable little shoulders you could scarcely imagine bearing the weight of being alone in a fenced-in camp in a foreign country. Here was a calm and professional trio of men discussing how best to use DNA samples from these children, without mentioning the most urgent need for matching families up was actually because they had tricked or forced those very families into separating. This separation was even possibly carried out by the very agents sitting in the room.

Had I stood up at that moment and said, "Sir, you're speaking openly about more efficient ways to get DNA from babies you've stolen!" I would have seemed insane, even though that was exactly what was happening, as hundreds of people listened, nodding. I wonder if those same people would intervene if they saw a stranger take a baby from her mother on the street.

I met some lovely people at the Alamo. I sat down to eat at a picnic table of retired agents and their wives and friends, introducing myself as I did. They showed me the best way to roll up tacos and told me stories of Marfa, Texas, before it was a conflicted art spot, back when it was literally a two-horse town. They looked out for me, a stranger at their table, and made sure my cup was full. I asked them about the significance of the Alamo, and they gave me a potted history. As with any battleground, there are different sides to the story. Theirs was that in 1836 the Texans who were holding out there against the Mexicans, whose territory they had captured earlier that year, were then treated horrifically by Mexico. They were massacred by the Mexican general, the notorious Santa Anna. Thinking about it, one woman looked troubled and urged me to understand how awful it had been, as if remembering it herself.

In context, the battle was one of many in a war that ended with the US annexing 55 percent of Mexico's territory and militarily occupying the remaining country between 1846 and 1848. The future president Ulysses S. Grant, who fought in the war, later called it "one of the most unjust ever waged by a stronger against a weaker nation." He compared

American aggression to that of the European monarchies, who continued their colonial rampaging for decades to come.

The Alamo is a historic site of struggle between Mexico and America, but it was originally in Mexico. Much of history omits that. In these older folks' minds there was no question of the significance of the grounds we were sitting in, and as the evening drew in and the low floral centerpieces (sponsored by ManTech—"Securing the Future") released their lovely honey scent, we talked about it. "You think of this as a place where there was huge brutality, by Mexicans? That's what it means when you say 'Remember the Alamo'?" I asked one of my tablemates, and they nodded yes.

Today, the violence between Mexico and the US is even more one-sided, and is not usually carried out in full view but rather deliberately obscured. The chaos and fear caused by the coronavirus have proved an ideal smokescreen for increasingly draconian treatment, including a March 20, 2020, order encouraging the immediate deportation of noncitizens arriving overland without valid documents. This came from the Centers for Disease Control and Prevention (CDC) and cited an obscure quarantine law from 1944 to justify the move on public health grounds. Tens of thousands of people, including children as young as ten traveling alone, have been deported since then. Despite complaints from the United Nations Refugee Agency, on May 19 DHS effectively ended asylum indefinitely, with a review every thirty days.

Another method of obfuscating the plight of migrants at the hands of the US is to physically remove the migrants from the country, even after they've made an acceptable request for asylum. Since the Migrant Protection Protocols (MPP), the "Remain in Mexico" program, went into effect in January 2019, more than sixty thousand asylum seekers from a variety of countries have been sent back to Mexico to await court dates in the US. Wealthier people among them can afford to stay in hotels and remain relatively safe, but many have fled poverty and certainly cannot afford a hotel. So they simply give up and turn back, or set up makeshift camps in Mexican border towns, where they're dependent on volunteers for basic supplies and regularly under threat of extortion, kidnapping, and physical and sexual violence.

The organization Human Rights First published a summary of more than one thousand cases of murder, torture, rape, and kidnapping against migrants sent back to Mexico under MPP. Despite this, on March 11, coincidentally the first day of the Border Security Expo, the Supreme Court upheld the policy. The news filtered through and was met with muted jubilation by the conferencegoers. Chief Rodney

Scott said MPP "restores the integrity to immigration." Sending migrants away, no matter how horrifying the consequences for both the migrants' lives and this country's moral compass, certainly makes Border Patrol's job a lot easier.

Almost one year later, President Biden began to undo some of the most violent anti-immigrant policies of his predecessor, including lifting the travel ban on thirteen Muslim-majority countries and African countries and reviewing, with the intent to end, that "Migrant Protection Protocol." He also created a task force to reunite families separated at the US-Mexico border and sent a comprehensive immigration reform bill to lawmakers. Significantly, President Biden halted construction of Trump's notorious border wall. I wondered if this was a signal that he was ready to consider taming the massive militarized machine that is the border security industry or if he, like Democratic presidents before him, would quietly continue to expand it. The border security industry contributed three times more to Biden's presidential campaign than to Trump's reelection campaign, and that is worrying. The Democrats consistently opt for a "smart wall," using technology to police the border, but both parties have expanded the physical fence too.

On March 7, 2020, a young Guatemalan woman fell backward from the top of an eighteen-foot-high span of steel mesh fencing and onto American ground in El Paso, Texas. Border Patrol agents called an ambulance, and she was rushed to hospital, but on Thursday, March 12, after a number of surgeries, she succumbed to her injuries. It feels wrong to describe only the nature of her death, but I do not know much about her life. I know she was thirty weeks pregnant and, despite delivery by C-section, the baby did not survive. I know that she worked as a social worker and was a former beauty queen, that she and her partner were hoping to support their family by moving to the US. I know her name was Mirian Estefany Girón Luna, and her partner was reportedly deported to Guatemala shortly after her body was repatriated.

Speaking to *The Washington Post*, Tekandi Paniagua, a Guatemalan consular official based in Texas, said the fact that the couple was attempting to get into the United States by climbing the fence was an indication of shifting migration dynamics at the border. "A year ago, during the height of the family migration surge, the couple probably would have tried to turn themselves in to seek asylum," he said. "This is a very worrisome trend. People are taking more and more risks, and they're losing their lives." The fence Ms. Girón Luna fell from was there to prevent migrants, and it did exactly that. Her life was not passively lost; she was "made to die" by US policies. She would not have been killed without those policies, or without the smiling men showcasing examples of bollards of various heights and finishes, one of them slapping a post and exclaiming, "This one is impossible to grip!" that very day in an air-conditioned hall at the Border Security Expo.

I left before the official end of the expo because I had gathered enough information to understand. I understood in a new, deeper way how little a life matters to a border. I understood that today, borders and the people who believe in them and enforce them are winning. But borders are not sustainable because the human instinct is to move when you need to, and in this century that need will only grow. I did not stay for the shooting competition that Friday. I flew back to New York and booked another flight the next day, back to Ireland where I grew up. The Irish government canceled all official celebrations of St. Patrick's Day on March 17, and that to me was like them shining a big green shamrock in the sky to signal us all home. I did not yet know that my adopted city would become the epicenter of the virus, and that the US would suffer more deaths per capita than any other country. I did not know that the virus would disproportionately kill Black and Brown people, but only because I did not yet know that what the virus would do was magnify what was already there. I had to go to the very edge of this country I loved and deliberately made my life in to learn what was already there: a disregard for how precious and important each person is, a profit-making exercise for a small number of people at the expense of millions of us. What was there was State violence against anyone the State did not want; this was heavily cloaked in laws and policies but still visible, dressed in neat uniforms with gold buttons and dark suits with muted ties.

One last thing: I was not serious when I said I bought the rifle and when I said I was wearing a pink cowgirl hat. The rest, I'm afraid, is true.

Death Tax

As a child, I loved a eucalyptus tree at the end of our garden. I mean, I truly loved it. I would admire its silvery jigsaw-patterned bark and climb its branches with my sisters to use its gray-green leaves as a hideout. Eucalyptus trees are not common in Ireland, and this one felt like a real and exotic presence within my family, with its menthol smell and great height. I forgot all about that tree until shortly after Donald Trump was elected president, and I was rushing to catch the train and heard a rustling from one of the trees that line the sidewalk in Brooklyn. When I glanced over, I realized it was a woman softly embracing a sycamore. Her hands didn't quite meet on the other side, but she was melted onto the tree and her eyes were closed in midcuddle. I looked away quickly, because it felt like a private moment. I had an urge to laugh. Little did I know that in a few short weeks I too would make a habit of sidling up to a sturdy maple and giving it a quick squeeze before running to catch the F train.

Although it was winter and the branches were bare, hugging that tree still felt good. No matter the season, a tree's trunk is solid, the bark rough and reliable. I was self-conscious at first; still am, a little. I try to make sure nobody is watching, and I don't hug it for very long. It's more like a lean or a quick check-in, and having touched something rooted I feel more rooted myself.

One autumn I made a trip to my friend Rachel's cabin in Vermont, a beautiful part of the country famous for its foliage. Predictably, I loved it. There were a great number of trees to hug, and just wandering among them was a balm. Russet red and glowing gold, stretching over hills. I felt just like Diane Keaton's character in *Baby Boom*, apart from the whole "inheriting a baby and sleeping with a vet" part, which sadly has yet to happen. I did make pies and tromp up a mountain and take a thousand dappled photos of the forest. On the car journey back I had the distinct feeling that I was leaving nature behind and stepping back into an artificial world. I hauled my bags of apples up the steps of my apartment building and turned to wave my friend off, and who did I see? The maple tree on my street, of course, and I could swear he was waving back at me. Pretty embarrassing for him since I was waving at Rachel, but still!

Being a grown-up isn't all it's cracked up to be. All the knowledge I gained made me forget that the city is nature too, and I am nature, and separations are simply illusory. Somewhere along the way I must have learned that trees are not living things to be treasured, but objects for humans to use. The term "tree hugger" is a pejorative, embedded in my brain so deeply that I can't recall the first time I heard it.

I know what is meant when someone is called a tree hugger: it's dismissive and ridicules the person, inferring they are an ineffectual and naïve hippie. It is supposed to mean a kind of pathetic figure with an embarrassingly emotional connection to an object. That's incorrect, and I've discovered that a big part of what is missing when we talk about trees, or the ocean or the planet, is exactly that: an emotional connection. The natural world is something *felt*. That rare eucalyptus tree, and what it felt like to hide in the branches there, was something I *felt* and never quite put into words until now. At the risk of stating the obvious: when sharing something I've felt, I need words. Nature is something we talk about and understand through words, especially as we get older and spend less time feeling what it's like to be up among the trees.

It is more than words we need to change; it's actually our

relationship with the planet and all the creatures and even "things" around us. Words are a good start, though, because language shapes thinking. The way we tell a story also creates the story.

Some words we have outgrown—"climate change," for example which was deliberately conceived to desensitize people to the magnitude of the looming disaster. Some words, we are stumbling toward—"the Anthropocene," for example, or "Martians," as in, should we all be planning for life as one? We must search for words that are clear as a bell, that won't seem up for debate. I'm far more comfortable in a library than in a jungle, and would rather get lost in a book. Words are my nature too, so I wrangle them in whatever way I can. It can feel hopeless to contemplate the enormity of the challenge that we are facing as we continue to destroy nature, despite relying on nature for our own survival. Something we do have control over are the words we use.

Learning how to talk about the age of extinction we are living and dying through has been a process for me. I cohosted a climate podcast for some years, and I am so grateful for what it gave me: access to lots of good information on what was happening to the climate, and also the space to figure out how to talk about it. Climate communication is political—everything we do is. Orwell wrote the following in 1946, and it's still true today: "In our age there is no such thing as 'keeping out of politics.' All issues are political issues, and politics itself is a mass of lies, evasions, folly, hatred and schizophrenia. When the general atmosphere is bad, language must suffer."

The atmosphere is bad, and language has suffered. This is no accident. Rising temperatures and sea levels, hurricanes, floods, fires—we all know of and many of us have experienced the violence of these climate crises. To lump them all under the benign-sounding "climate change" is baffling. At least it was to me, until I learned where that modest moniker for such awful and total chaos came from. In 2002, a Republican strategist named Frank Luntz wrote a memo. Luntz is familiar to many for his association with US politics and voter focus groups. He worked for Ross Perot and Rudolph Giuliani and is credited with shifting the frame from the term "estate tax" to "death tax." "Estate tax" sounds like it applies only to very rich people, which is and was always the case; it generally affects only the top 1 percent of taxpayers. Switching to "death tax" sounds like everyone will have to pay, since everyone will die. Republicans were able to drive up support for repeal using this neat trick. So when I say Luntz is a "communicator," what I mean is his entire professional purpose seems to be unmooring language from whatever unpalatable reality he is tasked with obscuring. This particular memo related to climate change and it pushed two big ideas. One was to communicate at all times that the science was not yet clear on what was causing global warming. "The scientific debate is closing [against us] but not yet closed. There is still a window of opportunity to challenge the science."

I get so furious when I read that sentence my breath thickens. From time to time I see Frank Luntz being a talking head on cable TV, billed as a communications expert. That is exactly what he is, and maybe that's the reason I'm more incensed by him than by the people who carried out his instructions. He understands the power of language and he used his gift with words to set this country firmly on a path of death and destruction. Many years later Luntz tried to put his filthy genie back in the bottle, but it was too late. By 2017 the bottle was smashed to pieces when the Skirball Fire threatened Luntz's Los Angeles home. Of course, neither he nor his house burned; in any case the wealthy are the most likely to survive climate catastrophes. The scare was enough for him to change tack and testify before the Senate's Special Committee on the Climate Crisis that he had been wrong in 2001, saying: "Just stop using something that I wrote 18 years ago, because it's not accurate today."

It wasn't accurate then either. And why would people

who benefit from the confusion he sowed ever stop sowing? Another part of his 2001 recommendation was for Republicans to stop saying "global warming" and start saying "climate change." Luntz advised, "While global warming has catastrophic connotations attached to it, climate change suggests a more controllable and less emotional challenge."

Republicans, including the then president George W. Bush, did just that, and then some. *The Guardian* reported that "the phrase 'global warming' appeared frequently in President Bush's speeches in 2001, but decreased to almost none during 2002, when the memo was produced." In swapping "global warming" for "climate change," the Bush administration helped to establish the latter as a catchall to describe something vague and broad. "Climate change" can mean any number of things to any number of people, and this looseness has been exploited by deniers and delayers. Sanitizing the language was step one, and it was followed by decades of destructive climate policy and rising carbon emissions. This rise was met with increasing global temperatures and a growing number of climate migrants. Taking the emotion out of words necessitates taking the anger out of suffering, but for the human race to survive this will take no small degree of fierceness.

The first tree huggers were incredibly fierce. The term was coined more than two centuries ago when 294 men and

69 women of the Bishnoi sect of Hinduism physically clung to the trees in their village in order to prevent them from being used to build a palace. The story takes a gruesome turn, when these tree huggers were killed by the lumberers who cut down the trees. Can you imagine putting your body on the line for a tree? In 1974 in Uttar Pradesh, India, a group of peasant women hugged trees, using their bodies as a physical barrier to protect them from foresters. This practice spread, culminating in the Chipko (meaning "to hug") movement, which forced deforestation reform and greatly helped to protect trees in the Himalayan region.

At my local park in Brooklyn, Prospect Park, there are three saplings, growing stronger each month. Those trees were planted to mark the spot where a man set himself on fire in April 2018. David Buckel, a civil rights lawyer turned environmentalist, self-immolated in an attempt to ring the alarm, to wake people up. "My early death by fossil fuel reflects what we are doing to ourselves," he wrote in an email to media. "Pollution ravages our planet. . . . Most humans on the planet now breathe air made unhealthy by fossil fuels, and many die early deaths as a result." His email ended with, "Here is a hope that giving a life might bring some attention to the need for expanded actions."

Today, deforestation is a leading cause of global warming. In 2010, together with agriculture, it accounted for about 24 percent of global greenhouse gas emissions. A report in *Scientific American* states that deforestation in tropical rain forests adds more carbon dioxide to the atmosphere than the sum total of all the cars and trucks on the world's roads.

One of the least discussed but, I suspect, most effective agents in the race to save ourselves from extinction is reconnecting to nature. When I hug a tree I get a tiny, blessed glimpse of the truth, which is that I'm a very small part of a gigantic ecosystem. David Buckel is often on my mind when I take walks in Prospect Park. He was right about man-made pollution ravaging our planet; everything he said is true. I'm not interested in derisive terms like "tree hugger" or "hippie" for people who care about the things he cared about. It's not silly or even illogical to hug a tree, but it is pure madness to blindly continue destroying our only home. I'm regularly surprised by how enmeshed I am in the ways we wreck this world of ours. *Hoping* will not change what's going to happen. I *hope* that Michael B. Jordan will fall in love with me and together we will move to an island and found a donkey sanctuary. But hoping won't make that happen—action will. Until I find out where he lives and muster up the courage to propose to him, there is little chance we will even form a relationship!

Being hope*less* is equally ludicrous. It is fashionable today to face doom with a nonchalant nihilism, but behaving as though the apocalypse is inevitable dismisses the hard work of many who are trying to prevent it. You must earn the right to be hopeless. Unless you have truly exhausted all of your options you can't truthfully claim hopelessness.

In a mess this big, if you want to claim hope, the only correct course is action. That shouldn't be so hard but, for me at least, it is. Curbing my own behavior feels almost ridiculous when I know that twenty fossil fuel companies are responsible for one-third of all carbon emissions. Knowing the political history and profitability of climate change denial, and having lived under the Trump administration for four years, which was almost laughably dedicated to endangering us all, I find it difficult to imagine I, just one person, could do anything. But it's even more difficult to ignore my own complicity. It's that discomfort that makes me act. That and Sadie, my pink-cheeked niece in Ireland who looked up at me the last time I visited and said, "Sometimes I wonder, is that moon following me?" Sadie is five years old. She deserves a fair chance at a healthy and safe life, just as every child does, even if they're not as cute as she is. We go on having children at the same time as we are wrecking their only home, which is really difficult to accept. So perhaps there needs to be a word for that, like paying it forward except you're not doing them a favor; you're making their lives worse. Owing it forward? Making your children pay your debts? How about "death tax"?

I did one small thing—I joined a credit union and posted a picture of my chopped-up Chase Bank cards on Instagram. Suddenly, all of my friends—and their friends—were clamoring to know how they could do the same. I broke the internet. It was exactly like the time Kim Kardashian released photos of her bare bottom except with taking constructive action to prevent total climate collapse. Everybody wanted to know how they could leave too, as if I had cracked some secret code that gave me agency over my own behavior. The thing is, I'd been meaning to leave for ages, ever since I learned about how Chase and other American banks invest their customers' money in the fossil fuel industry. At one point I called Chase and the customer service lady hung up on me when I asked her about the bank's deadly practices.

I wish I could have left then and there, but I wanted to pay off my credit card bill first. I owed Chase thousands of truly unnecessary dollars because my credit card had a mind of her own! She was trashy and lazy, always putting me into Lyfts instead of letting me walk or take the train. She loved nothing more than ordering food online instead of allowing me to cook, and would stay up late at night buying too many skin-care products on Amazon. The funny thing is, I never really agreed to all of that. I missed walking; walking calms me down. I like cooking, and I never worried about my skin until I started buying all those potions. It is also not lost on me that the things I spent money on—the real reasons I got stuck with Chase—took a heavy toll on other people, land, and animals.

Buying, taking, and using exhausts me and depletes everything around me, except the companies profiting from my behavior. One way to view it is that my credit card put me in a car driven by a person trying to get by in a punishing gig economy. Unlike Lyft drivers, public transport workers are unionized and paid a fair and regular wage and, of course, the carbon emissions are lower than cars. My old credit card made the food delivery app Seamless an easy choice too. But ticking the box that mockingly says, "Spare me the napkins and plasticware. I'm trying to save the earth," made me furious. So I cut her up and closed my account. They make it a little bit tricky, in that you have to sit in one of those fake offices in the middle of the bank with a sweaty twenty-two-year-old and tell them why you're leaving. I was abashed, facing the young manager in his terrible suit, answering when he asked the reason why I was leaving: "Um, because Chase funds fossil fuel companies and that is . . . bad." All my bravado had fallen away. "Okay, I'll type that in. Okay, awesome!" he said with no hint of reflection.

He worked for a company that was deeply complicit in the injustice that is climate change, and I gave them my money for years. I felt no rancor toward him or myself, understanding that it was just a pretty stable job, just a fairly convenient bank. I didn't feel smart or holy. I just felt lucky I had finally understood that I had some agency over small choices. I felt so light and free the day I left the bank, it was almost comical. As ever in my dark Irish brain, comedy and tragedy are forever chasing each other around in circles.

I'm not sure it's fair, the amount of rage I feel toward Frank Luntz and other wordsmiths who pave the road toward obliteration. Is it really too much to say that words nursed this age of extinction into being? Like Frank Luntz, I'm a Republican strategist. Sorry to let you down, but how else could I afford a home in LA? I'm joking! But what I do have in common with him is that language and storytelling are also my chosen form of communication. The Luntz memo illustrates the power of language. He advised a small number of people to stop using some terms and start using others, and the future of the entire planet and everybody on it moved in one direction. If George W. Bush had not prioritized capitalism over climate justice, where would we be today?

In 2018, the Intergovernmental Panel on Climate Change (IPCC) stated that carbon dioxide emissions would have to be cut by 45 percent by 2030 to keep the rise in global temperatures below 1.5°C. There is little hope of that happening. In July 2020, *Science* magazine reported on a landmark effort by twenty-five scientists measuring "climate sensitivity," and their predictions are dire. The assessment, conducted under the World Climate Research Programme, relies on three strands of evidence: trends indicated by contemporary warming, the latest understanding of the feedback effects that can slow or accelerate climate change, and lessons from ancient climates. They support a likely warming range of between 2.6°C and 3.9°C.

The devastation we are seeing now is just a trailer for a horror film, particularly when viewed through a climate justice lens. For every one degree the temperature rises, hundreds of millions of people will suffer. Their homes will be flooded or washed away, or their area will become an unlivable hot zone with a broken food and water supply. Women and children in the Global South will suffer first and worst. In the cities and coastal communities of the US, Black and Brown people and poor people will suffer first and worst. From a climate justice perspective, every reduction—large or small—in carbon emissions is worth the effort. Communicating this message is essential because language must translate into action, to spark mass behavioral change.

I'm hardly the first to worry about how language shapes

our thinking, and how telling stories creates stories. Writers like George Monbiot, Rebecca Solnit, and Eileen Crist talk regularly of the terms we use to reflect both the violence of some humans toward the planet and the beauty of this planet. Other scientists and scholars, like Robin Kimmerer and Glenn Albrecht, argue for new terms to be adopted instead of English words, either from Native languages or by innovating new ones. The writer Angela Carter stated, "Language is power, life and the instrument of culture, the instrument of domination and liberation."

A couple of years ago, I was a guest on a comedy and science panel discussion—a combination that works well because when you laugh your mouth opens, allowing information to float freely into your head. We were talking about the possibility of travel to Mars. The conversation had turned to how moving to Mars would be useful if and when we wreck our own planet.

James L. Green, a physicist who has since become the chief scientist at NASA, said he wants to send humans to colonize Mars: "As explorers, as Americans, this is what we do." The audience cheered and that's when something inside me flinched a little. There were the words—colonize, American, Mars. There was the context, the history, and the threat in each of those words. Obviously, there's the whole colonialism thing, which has historically been not that great for many of us. Also, there's the enormous resources we'd need to get to Mars. So far, only Matt Damon has made it safely there. Mainly, though, I balked at the thought of us marauding around the solar system instead of simply getting ahold of ourselves back here on Earth and working to prevent our own extinction.

Ghosting, in modern dating parlance, is when your beloved vanishes without explanation, having taken what he or she needed. Rhiana Gunn-Wright, a policy expert who helped shape the outline of the Green New Deal, says that humans are ghosting the planet. This joke is a perfect analogy. We're in this fabulous life-giving relationship with Earth, this ideal planet, but we're messing her around. We're using her and we're not answering her calls, and planning on leaving her for a cooler planet as soon as we figure out how.

The irony is that Earth is probably better off without us, and can certainly carry on long after we are gone. I can see her twirling into the future now, flaunting her revenge body made of lava and poisonous tides, completely inhospitable to us poor clowns. Then we'll be sorry. Well, we'll be dead, but I was raised Irish Catholic, so I believe it's possible to feel guilt well into the afterlife. Mars is a fantasy, a faraway and icy mistress beckoning us to leave the mess we've made and take our oxygen-starved chances with her. It is a seductive distraction from what ails us, not a viable solution. Government agencies from countries around the world, as well as billionaires and futurists, say that travel to Mars is an insurance policy, that they're working on a "planet B," but I don't buy that. Not just because I can't and will never be able to afford it. When we break something, we need to at least try to fix it.

What can any one person do? Scolding does come naturally to my thin lips, and I love to be right. But while I feel good after making someone feel bad—"Oh. Hmm. Is that a single-use plastic bottle?"—nothing is ever that simple. I mentioned I hosted a podcast on the theme of climate justice, and that I've learned a lot. Not one of the scientists or farmers or Native American activists I've spoken to has taken me aside and said, "Listen—'Maeve the Martian' has a nice ring to it; get on up there, girl!" Rather, I've learned that the way to prevent further climate catastrophe is much closer to home: personal behavior change combined with collective action and political progress. A conversation with Anne Poelina helped teach me that. She is a researcher at the University of Notre Dame Australia, a member of the Nyikina Indigenous community, and what is known as a traditional owner from the lower Fitzroy River. For many marginalized people, climate change isn't the first existential battle they've faced. Poelina's people and lands have faced enormous threats throughout the years, but she never left to pursue opportunity elsewhere. She has worked consistently and cheerfully to connect traditional ecological knowledge to Western science.

I've learned that despair is a luxury. Most of us can't plan an escape. We're also not willing to accept a dystopian future. The trip to Mars will take around nine months, assuming you make it through the meteors and cosmic radiation. You'd then have to figure out how to land, and that's when the work would truly begin: creating entirely new conditions that could allow you to survive. Even thinking about it a tiny bit seriously is an enormous feat of imagination and ingenuity. Instead, we could use that same imagination and ingenuity right here on Earth, right now, when we need it so desperately. Ghosting the planet is the worst thing we could do to ourselves. It's difficult to fully love the one you're with, though, if you don't see a future together. So I'm imagining a beautiful future for us and this planet, the happiest of marriages with coral and forests and honeybees all around. There will be no tut-tutting about where your take-out boxes end up because we'll have all calmed down and traveled back to a time when we sit around for hours and eat from real plates. We'll reminisce about that time we almost ruined everything but we're fine again now and, actually, aren't the butterflies getting to be a little much?

If what we are doing to our planet breaks your heart, let

it. I understand that "we" is not even or fair—I'm talking about the human race with the full understanding that some of us have been way more culpable than most. However, this is the predicament we are all in: all of our children face an uncertain future with varying degrees of protection. So, I repeat, if what we are doing to our planet breaks your heart, let it. Just make sure it breaks open wide enough to allow your imagination in. Change how you're thinking and talking, then you can shape the language and the story. Be the Luntz! The story will set in motion a series of events that were not previously possible because they were not spoken. The writer Rebecca Solnit does not mince words. "Climate change is global-scale violence, against places and species as well as against human beings. Once we call it by name, we can start having a real conversation about our priorities and values. Because the revolt against brutality begins with a revolt against the language that hides that brutality." This is a clear call to action for those of us in the words business; if climate change is violence, then we need to call it that.

The English language itself has pitfalls. Take the term "climate displacement." Climate crises caused by industrialized nations have ruined homes and livelihoods across the Global South, but industrialized countries do not refer to themselves as displacers; it remains a noun and never becomes a verb. If we in the Global North admitted to causing displacement, we would surely have to compensate in the form of climate reparations or open borders. That is . . . unlikely. The passivity of a language that relies on nouns helps to disguise our behavior. I learned from reading Robin Kimmerer that there are other languages, namely, her ancestral language, Potowatomi, that are largely made up of verbs.

"A bay is a noun only if water is dead. When bay is a noun it is defined by humans, trapped between its shores and contained by the world. But the verb *wiikwegamaa*—to be a bay—releases the water from bondage and lets it live. 'To be a bay' holds the wonder that, for this moment, the living water has decided to shelter itself between these shores, conversing with cedar roots and a flock of baby mergansers. Because it could do otherwise—become a stream or an ocean or a waterfall, and there are verbs for that, too. To be a hill, to be a sandy beach, to be a Saturday, all are possible verbs in a world where everything is alive."

The Potowatomi almost completely lost their language. For a century they were banned from speaking it by the English colonizers. Banning a language and imposing another can do more than destroy the original language. Since language is also a vessel of culture, in this case it can and did change our relationship to what is around us. Speaking personally (in English), I've become used to seeing other creatures and objects as something for me to use up and dispose of when it suits me. I don't have a sense of respect for them, or I do, but I quash it because it feels illogical or at least at odds with how most of society behaves, and certainly how we speak. Adopting this "grammar of animacy," as Kimmerer calls it, by incorporating more verbs into my language, either new or borrowed, could radically change my relationship with the planet.

It is clear that the new term for "climate change" needs to be a truthful descriptor. But should the violence of climate change be reflected in a new term for it, something like "climate murder" or "climate annihilation"? What if that term is just too much, and people really do have a "finite pool of worry" as described by researchers affiliated with the Center for Research on Environmental Decisions? Their work shows we are more likely to replace a long-term worry with something more immediate, and that a frightening term could push us away. Perhaps our brains simply do not have space to process another huge threat, particularly when it is perceived as further away.

If not fear, some emotion has a role to play in renaming "climate change." Certainly that's not an original thought. Philosopher and former earth science professor Glenn A. Albrecht has made the connection of human emotions to the planet his latest area of study, and his 2010 book, *Earth Emotions: New Words for a New World*, explores that in depth. In

June 2020 he wrote on his blog: "With new terms for our emotional relationship to the Earth, we are empowered and in a stronger position to reject the ecocidal past and create a better future."

In the past I have been told, "You're being emotional," in a negative way. It has been said to me in my personal and professional life as an insult that often incorporates my femaleness, and it's been said to me in a variety of situations, including discussions of climate. Hence, I'm planning to learn off the following quote from Dr. Albrecht's book: "The universe is a place of restless and endless motion. The word 'emotion' has its origins in the Latin *movēre*, 'to move,' and *ēmovēre*, 'to agitate, disturb.' I contend, therefore, that this makes the universe an 'emotional' place."

Should there be an entirely new term for climate change? Albrecht used New Latin to come up with a neologism not for climate change but for the emotions it elicits. "Solastalgia" is his word for "the pain or distress caused by the ongoing loss of solace and the sense of desolation connected to the present state of one's home and territory. It is the existential and lived experience of negative environmental change, manifest as an attack on one's sense of place." I like the word, but is it accessible? Is a Latin word really the best choice for a vibe we should all be able to instantly understand? George Orwell would not like "solastalgia" much. In his 1946 essay "Politics and the English Language" he writes, "Bad writers, and especially scientific, political and sociological writers, are nearly always haunted by the notion that Latin or Greek words are grander than Saxon ones." I feel like these types of words lend some credibility to an argument. However, using esoteric or grandiloquent words (like esoteric or grandiloquent) can serve to alienate others. It also relies on the old hierarchies (white, male, educated) that I've been conditioned to mimic. It's vital that I be as confident making that same argument in simple (or even emotional) terms.

Simplicity can also make new words or terms problematic. New words may flatten and sanitize just as much as or more than old ones, or they can distort an important message. There remains significant debate about the term "Anthropocene," which the National Geographic Society defines as "an unofficial unit of geologic time, used to describe the most recent period in Earth's history when human activity started to have a significant impact on the planet's climate and ecosystems." It has gained traction and is now commonly used in science, academia, and media discussion.

One scientist, Eugene Stoermer, invented this word, and another, Paul Crutzen, popularized it. In "On the Poverty of Our Nomenclature," Eileen Crist argues against using "Anthropocene." It's a relatively new term and a controversial one, and she concedes it's being widely used "partly because it is catchy and more seriously because it has instant appeal for those aware of humanity's impact on the biosphere." So "Anthropocene" is a successful new term to describe a horrifying new reality, but is it helpful? There are whole papers written on that, but Crist comes down with a resounding no, in that the discourse "refuses to challenge human dominion, proposing instead technological and managerial approaches that would make human dominion sustainable. By the same token, the Anthropocene discourse blocks from consideration the possibility of abolishing a way of life founded on the domination of nature."

The way the discourse obstructs our imaginations and our work toward a safe future reinforces the idea that there is some inevitability about climate crises. That is a serious problem from a climate justice point of view, ignoring as it does the fact that not all humans were and are bent on destruction. Humans lived on the planet for thousands of years before the Industrial Revolution without causing the massive damage we suffer today. Crist's other point needs to be taken too—the "Anthropocene" label cements us in place and erases the idea that another way is still possible today if humans manage to stop centering ourselves. At least the debate over the "Anthropocene" discourse is happening, but I would like to see the same debate over the term "climate change."

A new term, like "Anthropocene," can certainly help to make visible and comprehensible a huge and churning miasma like the effect humans have had on the planet since industrialized time, but it can also throw up new problems and compound old ones, so in coming up with new terms it's vital to consider the context, the framing, and the messenger, as well as the wording itself. I've thought about this in regard to the word "ecosystem," basically meaning a community of living things in a particular space. Albrecht, with his science background, understands why the word "ecosystem" came to be, along with "ecology" and "ecological." He writes, "They are useful terms in systems science but not so relevant to the expression of human emotions. Ecosystems are abstractions, as it is impossible to know where an ecosystem starts and finishes." Anna Tsing sees this abstraction as a danger because it plays into the human tendency to see ourselves as more important than every other species. "Species interdependence is a well-known fact—except when it comes to humans. *Human exceptionalism blinds us.*"

The climate movement doesn't need white saviors, or billionaires, or celebrities—at least, not only those people. It needs everybody. I will work to heal the language I can heal and commit to harm it no further. I try not to say "climate change" and give the Luntzes of this world the satisfaction of its obfuscation. I like "climate crises" because it's plural but when spoken aloud could be singular, and all climate crises are ultimately one crisis. It's urgent, it means something terrible is happening right now.

I'm not convinced it is the right choice from a climate justice point of view because it does not intimate who is most at risk, or who is culpable. That said, a crisis is also an inflection point. It means there is still time to change course and avert the worst. For now, that is true. Angela Davis has been quoted widely, saying, "You have to act as if it were possible to radically transform the world. And you have to do it all the time."

Eileen Crist reminds us that while it is important to know that human language and storytelling are crucial in understanding, it is also vital to consider there are other ways to communicate, many of which have been drowned out by the very noise of language and story. "These others have been de facto silenced because if they once spoke to us in other registers—primitive, symbolic, sacred, totemic, sensual or poetic—they have receded so much they no longer convey such numinous turns of speech, and they are certainly unable by now to rival the digital sirens of the dominant culture." Mars, a eucalyptus tree, an owl, a baby. We have to listen carefully for the registers they use to speak. At times, we need to be silent. I think back to the eucalyptus tree at the end of the garden, and me, a pale child with thick glasses, clambering up there and sitting in the fresh cool air whenever things got to be too much on the ground. What a simple refuge, what a natural alliance, what a gift.

The Innocents

Oh my God! I am fifty-four this year. I work hard and if I want to get married in the United States of America I have the right to do that. All we want to do is get married in America—it's my tax-paying right. It's my choice. Whether they're scamming us, using us, or not, it's our choice to bring them over here if we can afford them.

ANGELA DEEM, *90 Day Fiancé*, SEASON 7

The fact that I am unable to experience everything personally sometimes gets me down. I want to know other lives very badly. The most I can hope to do is try and mix it up a bit, perhaps train myself to appreciate rutabaga or learn Icelandic, but I will still fundamentally be stuck being myself. I will reveal to you now the best way I've come up with to inhabit the lives of others, my big effort in empathy: on public holidays, I watch *90 Day Fiancé*, for hours at a time. Independence Day and Thanksgiving are two holidays that allow me, as an immigrant with no family or traditions here, to make up new traditions. Those days began as spare ones, where everybody was off work and busy with friends and family, allowing me to do exactly as I pleased. So now I watch reality TV, an unthinkable indulgence on regular days, all the while feeling a peculiar tug between being enthralled and being horrified.

90 Day Fiancé is based on the K-1 visa, also known as a fiancé(e) visa. This is the visa a US citizen applies for on behalf of their betrothed when that person is a resident of another country and they want to come to America. The fiancé(e) visa allows that person to visit the US legally, but their status automatically expires after ninety days and cannot be extended, so they must marry or leave the country. The clock is built in: wonderful for a TV show, less so for exploring the complexities of a relationship between people from two different cultures who have not spent much time together. The pressure builds as the two try to understand each other. Like any couple, there are dozens of ways they fail to do so. Then there are extra ways for them to mess up because they're under pressure to make a decision and they're on camera and there are geopolitical forces at play. All of this messes with their balance as a couple and is, naturally, excruciating and very entertaining to witness.

I am a person writing a nonfiction book about America from my own specific perspective, and will no doubt grasp some things properly with a deep understanding. Other things will sail over my head as it's turned to look at something else that I'll no doubt imbue with too much meaning. I dare say that *90 Day Fiancé* could be the latter. But it's a TV show that can and does exist only here. Besides, it's more than just a TV show—it's a phenomenon! I urge you to take a look if you haven't already. There is drama and the possibility of romantic love; there are adorable people making terrible choices and creepy people making cunning choices, with talented story producers orchestrating the whole thing into vivid narratives. It's troubling at times, and some episodes feel exploitative. Most of the Americans on the show believe that they have a prize to offer and that prize is US citizenship. Usually they are slight outsiders; often they are unsuccessful people with little in the way of material wealth or security to offer another person. If nothing else, watching the show is a simple and enjoyable way to unlearn the myth of American exceptionalism.

The traditional tropes of reality television are there: tumultuous families living out chaotic patterns, unbelievable choices that manage to seem inevitable, and very poor acting. It's clear that some scenes have been scripted and others reenacted for the cameras. You will feel the common bewilderment as to why anyone would welcome a film crew and the potential derision of the world into their lives, but you'll never get a satisfactory answer. There's not much to gain, except a large following on social media; some participants eventually set up their own OnlyFans accounts. There is also the part I find most extraordinary, where the action is cut through with snippets of the participant sitting in a well-lit room with their hair and makeup done. Their role at that point in the show is to watch and narrate their own life, and they do so with a glazed look that vanishes from time to time as they realize what it is they've done. The thing that sets the entire *90 Day* franchise apart is the way it exposes simultaneously and ruthlessly both how shabby America can be and how completely unaware of that fact so many Americans are.

Angela Deem, quoted at the beginning of this essay, is a fifty-four-year-old hospice care worker from Hazlehurst, Georgia. She's been in the show since 2018, when she participated in season 2 of *90 Day Fiancé: Before the 90 Days.* Angela met her now-husband Michael Ilesanmi online, and then for the first time in Nigeria. Her trips there made for some extremely colorful scenes. She left the airport, sweating after a long and sleepless flight, in a shirt reading "Be Your #selfie" and was met by thirty-one-year-old Michael, whose shirt read "God Over Everything." They retreated to the Lagos Travel Inn, where she immediately began to fret about how to pay for their stay, splitting the cost between two credit cards. Once in the room, she grabbed at Michael's crotch and laughed hysterically, until she calmed down enough to present him with the gifts she had brought: a "MAGA" hat and T-shirt along with a bobblehead of Donald Trump. He held the statue gamely and tried on the T-shirt over his loose-fitting traditional garb.

It was pure chaos and hasn't stopped being chaos since then. After their initial meeting, when she'd returned to the US, she accused Michael of stealing from her, only to realize later it was a "banking error." Angela Deem has two daughters, Scottie and Skyla Deem, and six grandchildren. During the show, her older daughter, Scottie, was in prison for fifteen months for child abuse and statutory rape, but is now out on parole and on the Georgia sex offenders registry. Much of Angela and Michael's storyline hinges on her promise to him she was able to bear a child, and she immediately began trying to convince her daughter Skyla to carry any baby she may be able to conceive. This led to much confusion among Michael's family back home. In one episode set in Lagos, Michael's aunts and uncles sit around the table during a frank conversation about the couple's future. They look a little bewildered, a little amused, and even a little protective—not of their family member, but of this strange, rambling American who seems quite lost. Meanwhile, she too is making all sorts of assumptions about them, and none of them are great. She stays true to her "America First" convictions, and doesn't stop to consider how Michael's life in Nigeria is, compared to what she is offering him. They eventually married, in January 2020, but because of visa delays he has yet to make it to Hazlehurst, Georgia.

The default position taken by the Americans taking part in the show, including their usually suspicious family and friends, and I would wager many of those watching the show, is that everyone outside of America wants only to get in. It's not possible to quantify how true this is, but I believe it helps the series' popularity no end. However miserable your life is, if somebody wants in, doesn't that mean it's not as bad as you think? The franchise is hugely popular and, in any situation, you can usually find someone to talk to about it. The next flight you're on, why not ask the cabin crew if you can make an announcement? If they agree, loudly and plainly ask the passengers who among them watches *90 Day Fiancé* and I bet you dozens of hands will shoot up. You can then arrange where everyone is sitting to best facilitate a group conversation about your favorite moments! That's one way of testing the show's popularity. Another, easier way is to look at the numbers. It's consistently one of the top-rated shows on the reality channel TLC and has spawned at least ten spin-off shows, including *Before the 90 Days*, *Strikes Back*, *Pillow Talk*, *The Other Way*, and *Happily Ever After?* In an interview with *Vulture*, the network's president, Howard Lee, called the *90 Day* franchise "our version of a Marvel Comics Universe." The same article, published in August 2020, reported that although "more than 400 hours of *90 Day*–related programming have been produced so far— ratings for the shows keep going up. This summer *Happily Ever After* and *The Other Way* have been delivering monster Nielsen numbers, regularly outdrawing major broadcast- and cable-network shows in key demo groups, particularly younger women."

As much as I enjoy seeing myself as a special and differ- ent type of flower to the rest of the bunch, I see now that I am part of a "key demo group," to be fed and sold commodi- ties and become a commodity myself. Not only that, I also fit very neatly into how the others in that group behave, in that *this is my show!* How dull of me, to get a voyeuristic kick out of disastrously mismatched and intensely problematic relationships. Then I remember I have a special and different reason for watching the show to all the other "younger women" and I feel a lot better. *An intellectual exercise*, I say to myself.

After all, it is on TLC—the Learning Channel. I watch it to learn! Remember? I watch it to better understand this wild adopted country of mine! In some ways it's a reflection of my own experience here, arriving to this promised land of largess only to find it was something of a mirage. My learning curve was not dependent on an American citizen to allow me to stay or not, but some notes of familiarity do sound as I watch other foreign nationals arrive and learn that the glimmering city of their dreams is filled with rats, fresh fruit isn't on the menu for poor people, and their American hero has crippling credit card debt and no health insurance.

Participants sometimes threaten to "call immigration" on their boyfriends or girlfriends, and it's always ugly to see, particularly during the Trump administration. Despite the fact that immigrants commit fewer crimes than citizens, in 2017 the Department of Homeland Security set up a new office and a special phone line to "serve the needs of crime victims and their families who have been impacted by crimes committed by removable criminal aliens." That said, a blond woman calling the police on a Black man is another thing altogether. In season 6 of *90 Day Fiancé*, Ashley Martson did just that after discovering her new husband, Jay Smith, had cheated on her, stating, "I never filed his adjustment of status, so at this point he needs to go."

As Martson dialed 911 she summoned not only a force

that threatened Smith's safety and even his life but a specter that is centuries old now, that of white women in America weaponizing both their whiteness and their sexuality against Black men. From little Emmett Till to Christian Cooper, a gentle bird-watcher in Central Park, there is something twisted at work in America that often ends in devastation for Black men. In this case the police behaved themselves, interviewing both Martson and Smith, and they allowed him time to collect his things, checking that he had a ride. Martson remained livid in her piece to camera right after. "The cops were in agreement about my reasoning for calling and they agree that he has to go. However they couldn't get in touch with immigration because it is midnight. But they sent him on his way, and I'm going to contact them in the morning to pursue in getting him deported." Deportation is a form of slow and bureaucratic violence that, when fully understood, you would not wish on your worst enemy, let alone your twenty-year-old husband. But now you see? There I go, falling into the trap of believing that Martson was too innocent, too naïve, too . . . pretty to know what she was doing to Smith. Of course she knew just how devastating deportation is, which is why she was wielding it.

Those episodes are simply an X-ray that shows the bones of Americanness. They are illuminating for sure, but it's actually one of the spin-off shows, *90 Day Fiancé: The Other*

Way—where Americans go abroad and spend time in other countries—that gets to the marrow. It's difficult to comprehend what your country means and what its place in the world is, especially for Americans. There have been so many moments where their innocence has supposedly shattered—the Vietnam War, 9/11, Trump's election—yet it remains intact in many. I'm talking about white Americans, and the naivete of white Americans is a through line in the show. It's even played for laughs. One scene familiar to many fans is one in which fifty-four-year-old San Diego native "Big Ed" Brown visits the Philippines. He goes there to see his twenty-three-year-old girlfriend, Rosemarie "Rose" Vega, and is openly horrified by the conditions she lives in, recoiling in terror at a bucket and hose for a shower. She compares him to a baby, but of course he isn't a baby. His innocence is a stand-in for American innocence and it conceals a darkness. Americans have thrown their power around the world, yet the havoc they've wreaked is matched by white America's naivete. I doubt Big Ed knew that the US had colonized the Philippines for half a century, that it changed immigration laws specifically to disallow people from there to become citizens, that Filipino veterans who fought for the US in World War II had to wait decades for their families to legally join them in the country for which they'd risked their lives. Big Ed was frightened and judgmental that his hot young girlfriend didn't have indoor plumbing. He saw himself as her rescuer, a white savior who should be repaid with a lifetime of grateful companionship. What he did not see was that he and his compatriots trail along after a totally unaddressed, therefore potent, history of American exploitation and oppression of the Philippines.

Many Americans have little to no idea of the power dynamics at play inside their own nation, let alone the tidal waves of chaos it has unleashed around the planet over the past two centuries. It's ironic that there is a test for immigrants to become citizens, with answers many citizens don't know. Take it from me, a noncitizen: there is much to learn from the naturalization test, one of the final hurdles an immigrant must clear in order to become a citizen.

It's pretty tough, actually, particularly the new and expanded version of the test that President Trump proposed in the waning days of his administration. The test has traditionally been made up of civics questions about American government and history. Just getting to the test usually means you've made it through an obstacle course involving reams of paperwork, thousands of dollars in lawyer and government fees, years of legal residency, a biometrics appointment, and an English proficiency test. One of President Biden's early actions was to revert to the older test, with fewer questions than Trump proposed. The questions come in the form of an oral test where an officer from US Citizenship and Immigration Services (USCIS) asks the would-be citizen to answer ten of the one hundred civics questions; if she gets six right, she passes. After that, all she needs to do is pick up her paperwork. Then she can pledge allegiance to the flag and decide which season of *90 Day Fiancé* to watch to truly understand this complex nation.

The Naturalization Act of 1906 first decreed that citizens-to-be must speak English, and while English is not the official language of the United States, most immigrants today still have to pass an English proficiency test; further, the civics test is only carried out in English. I'm a native English speaker, but I still find some questions difficult to understand. And unlike in the study guide online, the questions are not multiple choice. That means that one day, if I get to take the test, I will have to try to keep a straight face as I look into another human being's eyes and try to answer the question "Why is the electoral college important?" Some people have an easier ride. If you are sixty-five or older and have twenty years of permanent residency under your belt, you are required to answer fewer questions. This makes me feel better about the substantial errors made by the sixty-six-year-old senator-elect from Alabama, Tommy Tuberville. In an interview in *The Alabama Daily News*, Mr. Tuberville got the three branches of the federal government wrong and misidentified the reason the United States fought in World War II. To be fair, Mr. Tuberville played football for a long time. It is my understanding that this extremely American game involves repeated bashes to the head, which are bound to knock some civics out.

I spoke to an Irish woman about her experience with the test. "It's just really punitive to people that don't have advanced degrees and it's not in their first language," she told me. She said she was not worried about passing her own test when she took it in 2020, on October 7, to be precise. It was the shorter and simpler version. Plus, she is a high school history teacher. Originally from Ireland, Ms. Hanlon Shook lives in Poughkeepsie, New York, and in past years used the USCIS questions to quiz her high school students as she waited her turn to take the real thing. "The idea was, if you weren't a citizen, would you pass this test? And a lot of them wouldn't."

Her turn finally came during a pandemic, so the USCIS officer brought her into a room with an iPad, and then he went to the room right next to hers and conducted the interview virtually. She got 100 percent of the questions right, and on October 23 she was presented with her citizenship papers and a small American flag during a drive-through ceremony in a parking lot beside the Albany airport. The next day, she told me, she voted in the presidential election.

One day I hope to do the same, so I'm taking practice tests when I can. This one caught me out. "What is Alexander Hamilton famous for?" He's famous for his cool ponytail and for being a breakout star on Broadway, right? Wrong. Apparently he's famous for being "one of the writers of the Federalist Papers." Not sure what those are, but they sound serious. Another one is "Name one example of an American innovation." Voodoo-flavored Zapp's chips spring to mind, as does unearned confidence. However, neither is included in the list of acceptable answers. Instead: lightbulb, skyscrapers, and landing on the moon.

Hernan Prieto is the citizenship program coordinator at Irish Community Services, a nonprofit in Chicago that provides immigration and social services to immigrants of any nationality in the Midwest. Part of his job is preparing immigrants for the civics test. Unlike Senator-Elect Tuberville, his students usually get the question about the branches of government right. They are also familiar with some of the names on the test, he told me. They know who Martin Luther King Jr. is and why he is important. Dates trip them up, though. A green card holder from Argentina, Mr. Prieto hopes to apply for naturalization next year, and he told me he appreciates what he learns alongside other immigrants. Most crucially, studying civics informs would-be Americans of what they stand to gain and what they need to give if they hope to live up to this nation's earliest motto. They learn that too: it's "E Pluribus Unum," or "Out of many, one." They learn that equality is promised by the Constitution, that nobody is above the law, and that it is a civic duty to vote.

Mr. Prieto treasures that knowledge but is not convinced that the test itself is helpful. "I don't know that we need to have a formal test. What is important for a new citizen to know are their rights and their responsibilities. That is what levels them with other citizens." I agree with him and wonder, does there really need to be a test? Particularly when it is so skewed and barely scratches the surface of the real America? I must sound like a rudely critical guest when I talk about America. I don't mean to, and I continue to live here, which serves as evidence that, just like many Americans before me, I love the place. Despite its chaotic energy and destructive patterns, I would be happy to stay and even to become a citizen.

In her brilliant book *Notes on a Foreign Country: An American Abroad in a Post-America World*, the writer Suzy Hansen says that, at least in the beginning, immigrants could have done with stricter conditions on citizenship. Speaking of the last time great waves of white people entered the country through Ellis Island in the last century, she suggests the following: "They should have gotten a months-long education on the Americans' destruction of its Indigenous population, on its history of slavery, on its persecution of darker-skinned immigrants, on its invasion of and occupation of Cuba and the Philippines—and later, on its vast and endless empire—and they should have been made to swear that they accepted this ugly American history as their own, that they vowed to take responsibility for it and its repercussions, and that they promised to protect nonwhite peoples as much as they protected their white selves—forever. This vow should have been the price of American citizenship. Because clearly something did go wrong in America. Americans had been bound to myth, not history."

Easy for me to point fingers, but in truth I too was long bound to myth. I wanted to be a writer in New York, and was willing to quash any misgivings I had about how or what allowed me to sail on in and do just that. In 2014, the first year of my life in the United States, I used "being new" as an excuse for everything. Being new, coupled with my Irish accent, helped smooth over a number of faux pas, including that one time when I pronounced the "x" in "faux pas" and my coworker thought I was cursing at him. I dived into this American adventure happily, learning as I went, comfortable in the knowledge that I'd arrived in a nation of immigrants and really, aren't we all just figuring it out?

Giddy at the prospect of a brand-new holiday, I prepared for my first Thanksgiving dinner at a friend's house. Was it true there would be sugar in the potatoes? Should I mutter "hut hut hut" continuously throughout the football game or just every now and then? And what to bring? I meandered into Paper Source and picked up some table decorations, a cute DIY teepee pack, and some funny paper headdresses, some shaped like Pilgrims' hats, some shaped like feathers. Turned out the potatoes were fully candy, nobody says "hut hut hut" ever, and making teepees and feather headdresses together was the perfect icebreaker. That afternoon of crafting and food turned strangers into friends. Much like, I imagined, the very first Thanksgiving, when white settlers and Native people put aside their differences to collaborate on cranberry sauce recipes and generally had such a blast that all was forgiven.

You already know that I was mistaken. In 2016, I was making a podcast about immigration and devoted one episode to how immigrants spend Thanksgiving. Researching that episode got me thinking that we're not really a nation of immigrants after all, since there were Native people here for many thousands of years before those first European settlers, and Native people are, of course, still here.

I spoke to Gyasi Ross, a writer and attorney from the Blackfeet Nation, and told him about my first Thanksgiving, with those paper teepees and headdresses. "Yeah, that's horrible," he said, and explained. "The problem with images like that is they capture a particular time and keep us in that time." It's not just casual Paper Source shoppers who encounter cutesy images that bolster this warped view of history. Andi Murphy produces and hosts *Toasted Sister*, a fantastic podcast about Indigenous food. She is Diné (Navajo) and lives in Albuquerque. As a child, she said, she did those same craft projects at school—"the buckskin-clad Indian cartoons with beads and feather headdresses"—and thought little of it. That changed when she got to college. "A lot of Native kids are pretty angry when they go to college and get themselves into American Indian studies class and they learn all this truth about everything and they realize, like, 'Really? All of this was a lie?' Thanksgiving was part of that." Now, she feels her anger rise when her little cousins bring the same artwork home. "I get angry about all the injustices and atrocities that my people, and all Native people, have gone through, and that's not changing." I felt so dopey, an oblivious trespasser, not a clue about where I really was. That innocence is fine for children, but I'm an adult, and as an immigrant I chose to live here, so I want to understand as much as I can about this place I call home.

Back in 1993, an irate strawberry blond by the name of Donald Trump testified in front of Congress and made unfounded allegations that organized criminals were about to infiltrate casinos in Connecticut run by his competitors, the

Mashantucket Pequot tribe. How did he go after them? He questioned their authenticity, because they did not conform to a stereotype. "They don't look like Indians to me." Representative George Miller responded, "Thank God that's not the test of whether or not people have rights in this country or not, whether or not they pass your 'look' test." He may have thanked God a little early on that one.

In September 2018, President Trump's administration decided to reverse an Obama-era ruling placing land in trust for the Mashpee Wampanoag, the tribe whose ancestors sat and ate with the settlers during that first Thanksgiving back in 1621, the tribe that helped them to survive. The Mashpee Wampanoag had rallied in Washington, DC, lobbying Congress to protect those land rights and uphold their sovereignty. They are trying to hold on to just half of one percent of what was once theirs. I'm floored; how did I not know this? jessie little doe baird, the vice chairwoman of the Mashpee Wampanoag Tribe, was not surprised I hadn't heard. "It's so damn ironic, the treatment of Indigenous people is like this dirty little secret that a family has."

I'm thankful I get to learn these secrets, to get some clarity about this place I call home. I blunder around and learn as I go and am thankful for the education I'm receiving because isn't America fascinating? As the country convulses in an effort to remake itself, and lurches forward with a resurging civil rights movement, I can't take my eyes off the place. Each July fourth there's a national holiday for Independence Day, marking the anniversary of the 1776 adoption of the Declaration of Independence. This document is quite gorgeous in its aspirations, written by the representatives of 2.5 million people in just thirteen colonies and absolutely trashing the despotic British regime. They refuse to be governed by the British for a moment longer, and this right of the people to emancipate themselves and form their own government is surely a worthy event to celebrate. Of course, as with everything in a nation founded on genocide and chattel slavery on the one hand and "Life, Liberty and the pursuit of Happiness" on the other, it is not that simple. As with many American holidays, like Thanksgiving and Columbus Day, Independence Day must be critically scrutinized to be fully understood.

To help with this I look to two Americans who have both, at various times throughout history, been vilified and valorized. The first is Thomas Jefferson, one of the signatories of that cherished document, a man who would go on to become the nation's third president. As he lay dying half a century after signing the declaration, he described what it meant to him in a letter. "May it be to the world, what I believe it will be . . . the signal of arousing men to burst the chains . . . and to assume the blessings and security of self-government. That form, which we have substituted, restores the free right to the unbounded exercise of reason and freedom of opinion. All eyes are opened, or opening, to the rights of man. . . . For ourselves, let the annual return of this day forever refresh our recollections of these rights, and an undiminished devotion to them."

Glorious, isn't it? Thomas Jefferson wrote that from Monticello, his five-thousand-acre plantation where 130 enslaved people worked at any one time. According to the property's archives, Thomas Jefferson enslaved over six hundred human beings throughout the course of his life. Not only did he profit from their labor, he profited from buying and selling them. Female slaves had no legal right to refuse sexual advances from their owner, and Jefferson fathered at least six children with an enslaved woman named Sally Hemings. He also wrote, unsurprisingly, that he suspected Black people were inferior to white. It is crucial to understand this horrifying context when reading the Declaration of Independence. It is important to question whether or not this reality makes the entire document a sickening joke.

Frederick Douglass seemed to think so and he was more qualified than most, being born as he was into slavery and possessing one of the greatest intellects to ever emerge from America. On July 5, 1852, at an Independence Day celebration he'd been asked to speak at in Rochester, New York, he scathingly asked his predominantly white audience, "Do you mean, citizens, to mock me, by asking me to speak today?" He was explicit in his condemnation of the holiday. "This Fourth of July is *yours*, not *mine*. *You* may rejoice, I must mourn." He followed up with some of his most damning and righteous words, that still today will stop you in your tracks.

"What, to the American slave, is your 4th of July? I answer; a day that reveals to him, more than all other days in the year, the gross injustice and cruelty to which he is the constant victim. To him, your celebration is a sham; your boasted liberty, an unholy license; your national greatness, swelling vanity; your sound of rejoicing are empty and heartless; your denunciation of tyrants brass fronted impudence; your shout of liberty and equality, hollow mockery; your prayers and hymns, your sermons and thanks-givings, with all your religious parade and solemnity, are to him, mere bombast, fraud, deception, impiety, and hypocrisy—a thin veil to cover up crimes which would disgrace a nation of savages. There is not a nation on the earth guilty of practices more shocking and bloody than are the people of the United States, at this very hour."

It was more than a decade after Douglass made that speech, years that saw a bloody civil war and the eventual abolishment of slavery, more than four hundred years after its brutal beginnings. And yet today, when I read his speech again and substitute "American slave" with "African American," his words ring absolutely true. To witness the gross injustice and cruelty Douglass spoke of almost two centuries ago, we need only fast-forward to today and see with our own eyes any number of police officers attacking and killing Black people in public, or look at how life expectancy is set by postcode and Black and Brown people have been redlined into the poorer ones. Douglass referred to America's denunciation of tyrants as "brass fronted impudence." Hearing President Trump's threat to turn the military loose on his own citizens, a threat made outside the White House in June 2020 as police fired rubber bullets and tear gas at peaceful protestors gathered there, teaches us that this hypocrisy lives on too. Douglass's parting shot, about "the shocking and bloody practices" carried out by America, translates easily to the systemic oppression of Black and Brown people today.

Huge progress has been made since the days of Douglass and Jefferson. But compared to a white person, a Black person in America today is more likely to be shot by the police, to be arrested, to be jailed, to live in poverty, to be negatively affected by climate change, to die in childbirth, to die of COVID-19, and to die young. None of this is by chance; this is not an arbitrary set of tragic realities, rather it is the logical result of hundreds of years of white supremacist policies coupled with the insatiable neoliberal brand of capitalism adopted by America these past three decades. Living here, it was easy to be dismayed at such a seemingly inevitable situation, until recently. I count myself incredibly lucky to live here during the largest social justice movement the nation has ever seen.

#BlackLivesMatter was founded in 2013, following the acquittal of the man who murdered Trayvon Martin, a Black teenager. Three Black women—Patrisse Cullors, Alicia Garza, and Opal Tometi—created the umbrella group alongside the social media clarion call to "explicitly combat implicit bias and anti-Black racism and to protect and affirm the beauty and dignity of all Black lives." This must be done, they stated, "through a lens of race, gender, sexual orientation, and gender identity." The movement cut its teeth in the 2014 Ferguson Uprising, which continued for more than a year after a white police officer there shot Michael Brown, a Black teenager. BLM organized and strategized and showed up ready for this moment in America, this moment catalyzed terribly by the videoed police killing of George Floyd.

Wouldn't it be the sweetest of ironies to see Independence Day come full circle, to witness one year's celebration transformed from a tired roll call of hollow lies into an actual attempt to snatch that liberty mentioned in that long-ago declaration? In a way, the Declaration of Independence predicted this revolt against white supremacy; you need only read its first few lines to see. "When in the Course of human events, it becomes necessary for one people to dissolve the political bands which have connected them with another, and to assume among the powers of the earth, the separate and equal station to which the Laws of Nature and of Nature's God entitle them, a decent respect to the opinions of mankind requires that they should declare the causes which impel them to the separation." BLM has declared the causes, and Black Americans are leading the charge toward a nation that resembles the one those slave-owning white men alluded to in their words but never their actions. It's a thrilling time, echoing other moments in history where that change seemed within the country's grasp, but all the more exciting because it's happening right now, and unlike the past, the future is not yet written.

You know how countries have slogans, like Thailand is the "Land of Smiles"? That seems like a lot of pressure on citizens and tourists alike. An entire land of constant smiles? Even when you have lower back pain or you've just been served surprise divorce papers: Smile! Did you know that America's last attempt at a slogan was 2016's "All within your reach"? Of course, we're unable to say it with a straight face now. "It's aspirational," we murmured beneath our masks in the COVID-filled days, wincing as the country isolated and dipped further and further down in the world's estimation. At that time, the list of countries opening their borders to Americans had never been shorter. Ireland, unlike many others in Europe, was still allowing Americans in. I went to Ireland when the pandemic started, figuring it would be safer. It was.

However, I missed my home and my life and mainly Shake Shack, so I decided to come back to New York. It wasn't easy, because of the travel ban the United States had put in place on people coming from Europe. This obstacle was new to me. An Irish passport is a powerful one that usually grants me admission to most parts of the world, and an American visa like the one I have in my passport is an equally rare and precious thing. Suddenly, though, doors were being slammed shut and gates locked tight. I decided to return through Canada. I applied for and got my visa waiver online within minutes. I flew to London but was not allowed on the connecting flight to Toronto. It turned out Canada had an extensive travel ban too; Canadians were just too polite to shout about it. Between the jigs and the reels, as we say in Brooklyn, I had to come through Mexico. Not just transit through—I had to stay there for fourteen days, which I did. This itinerary was not my choice and certainly not logical, but that's what the travel ban did; it forced me to take two extra long-haul flights, as well as holding me squarely in the beautiful and resilient Mexico City, which at that time was a hot spot experiencing record-high levels of the virus. I was so grateful they let me through, and in the end, I made it back to New York, flying over the land border that was all but closed to those seeking asylum.

I wondered what would happen to the *90 Day* franchise when most people were stuck in their place of origin. I didn't need to worry. They were perhaps the only group of people who kept right on doing their thing during that whole pandemic year. While most other TV productions had to shut down, a spin-off show called *90 Day Fiancé: Self-Quarantined* appeared with incredible speed. The participants taped themselves. As TLC's Howard Lee told *Vulture*: "What we found fascinating was how quickly they adapted. Even when there was not a crew there, without an audio person, without a camera operator, without somebody running cables or lighting over there, they were able to move very nimbly. We were quite stunned. I was flabbergasted that we could make so much content out of people just in their homes. We turned something around in three weeks, which is a whole entire series of *90 Day Fiancé: Self-Quarantined*, and that worked out really well for us." I watched a couple of episodes. The happiest contributor seemed to be twenty-two-year-old Fernanda, who is Mexican and living in Chicago.

Her marriage to an American had lasted just six months, then they separated. She filmed herself just after her divorce came through, saying: "I feel relief. I feel free. I feel ready to eat the world." This was juxtaposed with footage of her making a protein shake. She was dating again, virtually. She sat in front of her screen for a virtual date with an ex–football player who opened strong: "Mexican food is my favorite. Maybe you can teach me how to salsa dance." Fernanda did not seem bothered by his lax approach to South American cultures, confiding to the camera later: "He has everything I like in a guy. I can't wait for this quarantine to be over when I can have a real date with him and be physically touching his muscles." Aside from Fernanda's charming greed for the world, much of the rest of the series resembled much of life during the pandemic—boring and sad. I particularly did not want to watch the couples who were kept apart by the necessary travel restrictions, because while they stand some chance of being together in person one day, so many never will.

I remain rocked by how something as physically flimsy as a passport can serve to divide human beings up into two groups, the powerful and the powerless. Of course, this is not news to billions of people around the world. My inconvenient route home was hardly a taste of the reality lived by most people alive today, it's just that now this bad luck is finally going around. During the 2020 pandemic and for who knows how long, Americans have been banned from visiting most of the rest of the planet. Perhaps now that American passports have stopped working and this nation-state is no longer on top, more Americans will understand the injustice of the entire system.

Now that more of us are seeing and living the constricting and dangerous reality of those artificial distinctions, surely we need to change them. It is the person, as in the human being, the vulnerable creature no different to any other, that is sacred: not their paperwork. Americans are learning that now; some are learning it when they fall in love with someone from another country on a reality show, some are learning it when they can't vacation in Switzerland for the first time in years, and some are learning it when they try to take shelter in Mexico when a huge climate catastrophe hits Texas, a state they happen to represent in Congress. Whether these Americans can learn what their still powerful country means within the ecosystem of the planet, and understand what their country does and what it could do? That remains to be seen.

New York,
Fair or No Fair

There are, of course, a hundred New Yorks.
A thousand, perhaps a million.

MARJORIE HILLIS

The attraction and revulsion I have for New York drives me mad; that's how I know I'm a New Yorker. The city remains oblivious to our slavering and our seething alike. New Yorkers are the scrambling little upstarts, and New York is the Don Draper in an elevator staring straight ahead, saying, "I don't think about you at all." Of course, this makes me love the place even more desperately. On one of my visits here, years before I made it my home, I bought a book titled *New York, Fair or No Fair: A Guide for the Woman Vacationist* written in 1939 by Marjorie Hillis, an editor at *Vogue* magazine. The book is written in an authoritative tone and sets out "a chart for an Extra Woman who, like myself, likes to get as much as she can of the flavor of the city she visits, and as much as she can of the fun of it, in a limited time and on a limited budget, but with no limit whatever to her interest and her eagerness." It includes advice on what to bring, who to tip and how much, and even where to rent a male companion if you so wish.

I found the book in Bonnie Slotnick Cookbooks, a store in a fairy-tale cottage tucked away on East Second Street at the bottom of a redbrick town house. Daffodils nod along the patio in spring and, inside, shelves are packed full of vintage cookbooks and tables are laden with quaint accoutrements. Neighbors drop by with their little jacketed dogs and rummage through new arrivals. The self-identified "spinster-proprietress" Bonnie Slotnick herself sits behind the counter and happily obliges customers with in-depth knowledge about her books, as well as advice on what to do in the city, handing tourists maps of the neighborhood and generally acting like a character in a Nora Ephron movie. Photographs are forbidden. As I mentioned, I was a tourist myself the first time I visited the store and bought the book, back when the store was located in the West Village. I interviewed Bonnie Slotnick for a piece I was writing on small business in the

city, and she told me that she lost the lease on her first loca-
tion, calling it "a brutal experience." With ever-rising rent
and predatory landlords, it's extraordinarily difficult to keep
a small business afloat in New York, and Slotnick knows
she's the exception to the rule. Her current landlords heard
about her loss in 2014 and immediately called her up, offering her a rare deal on the commercial space in the house they
grew up in—a ten-year lease at a fair rent. "The store pays
for itself and a little bit more," Slotnick tells me. "I'm not
ambitious. I'm not looking to be more famous than I am.
I'm about as famous as I can stand." Perhaps this is the
magic that makes the store feel like a fairy tale, and has
made me love my first-edition copy of *New York, Fair or No
Fair* even more. The World's Fair referred to in the title has
long since ended, but I hope, as Marjorie Hillis did, to in-
troduce you to my version of New York. And sorry for the
spoiler, but I don't want to mislead you—I don't know where
to rent a male companion.

I learned how to drive in New York City and passed my
test in Red Hook, Brooklyn, among grimy waterfront ware-
houses. As I learned, many other drivers on the road terrified
me. On my third lesson, someone shot through a stop sign
in front of me and missed my car by a whisker. I had braked
and I was lucky. After I regained the power of speech I asked

my instructor, "Could you tell me exactly what to do so that what just happened back there never happens again?" He gently suggested I look at the road, so I serenely faced forward again, my heart still hammering in my chest. Then he told me, in his Russian accent, "There is nothing you could do differently in the future, you can only trust that everybody else on the road does the right thing, that's it." An unsatisfactory response, but the only truthful one.

I could not control and cannot control what anybody else does on the road and even if I did everything right, I could still get absolutely crushed. In that way, obeying the rules of the road feels quite like obeying the rules of a democracy. You do your part and hope everyone else does theirs. If liberal democracy is the end goal for the evolution of the United States, which most act as though, if not say that, it is, then the deal has to be that each one of us needs to take responsibility for everyone else. In a car—and in a society like ours—we know we must obey the rules of the road, but more than that, we have agreed, theoretically, to take some measure of care of one another. If we fail to do that, this whole thing will stop working. There will be rage and nasty pileups, and people could even get killed. Yet here we are, in this hyperindividualistic place where when you're doing well you're told you're a hero. That isn't true, of course, and neither is the rusty and scratched-up side of the same coin:

the fiction that when you're doing badly, it's completely your own fault. What I'm trying to say is, even after I passed my driving test, I took the train.

On the subway I mind my own business, like any good New Yorker. Unless I'm in a bad mood, like that cold day when nobody was emailing me back and my jeans were too tight and I was late for a meeting I didn't want to go to anyway and this kid turned his profane rap music up to full volume on the platform. Black and Brown teenagers are often overpoliced in public spaces, but this kid was as white as Post Malone. I spotted a much smaller child a few feet away: perfect. "Turn that off," I boomed at the teen, modeling my voice on that Theranos scammer. "Can't you see there is a small child over there?" I didn't care about the child—she was probably listening to a podcast about murder, anyway—I was just cranky. But more than that, I didn't need anyone breaking the social contract we all silently enter into when we disappear beneath the ground.

Swiping that MetroCard or jumping that turnstile admits us into a subterranean world with complex rules. The rules I care about are not written down, rules like "Don't spread your giant important legs," "Do not bother each other," and "Keep your eyes on your phone screen at all times." Sometimes, when I take a break from staring at mine and stretch my crooked little neck up to see how many stops I have left,

I accidentally lock eyes with someone else sneaking a sip of reality. We frown at each other and go back to our screens, as it should be.

Every now and then, paying attention can be wonderful. I looked out the window of the B one afternoon and watched as a woman who had been sitting opposite took two steps onto the platform, then looked at her hand, then whipped her head back at the train with horror. Right then the man sitting beside me lunged at the man opposite me. I got a terrible fright and thought he was attacking him, but he was reaching down because he'd spotted a diamond ring on the floor. He then leapt toward the door and handed the ring to the frantic woman, whose face broke into a huge smile. It was like she was getting proposed to all over again, except this time by a stranger speckled in cement. He apologized to the guy he'd jumped at and we all shared a laugh and it felt extremely good. Thirty-five minutes later (I was going way uptown to the Natural History Museum), I waved goodbye to the speckled man and he made a "who the hell are you?" face. He'd gone into his train zone and forgotten we'd shared that moment, and that made it perfect.

International Express: New Yorkers on the 7 Train is an excellent read, chronicling as it does the busy Queens subway line along which eighty languages are spoken. The authors observe that the subway really can teach us to accept each other. They note that by riding the train together, New Yorkers born here or immigrants new to the country end up making slight changes to their personal values and their attitudes, creating what they call a "practical cosmopolitanism."

One in three New Yorkers are immigrants. Many more are the children of immigrants, and public transport is where we all get close. It's the portal to each of our neighborhoods. While practical cosmopolitanism becomes us, our city is hardly a bastion of equality. New York City is reportedly home to more billionaires than any other city around the world, over one hundred of them. We also have one of the poorest counties in the whole country, the South Bronx, where poverty devastates around 35 percent of the people living there. The subway service has gotten steadily worse in the years I've lived in New York. That has nothing to do with me, I swear; it's a coincidence. The subway is a symbol of what local and state government actually values and supports, and because they do not support the subway—a populist service—it's suffering badly, with ancient infrastructure and growing delays. The fall in ridership and the brutal budget cuts following the pandemic are slowly killing the subway. It's obviously a mess, and yet! The subway is essential, and along with its failings it has held on to enough liberating glory to keep me coming back. It is simply the best technology I know for experiencing the city.

I needed it when I took a job in a writing room, one that made me a commuter for a couple of months. There were ten other writers, and we were stuck in a coworking space in Bushwick. The building was new, sleek looking, and not quite in keeping with the rest of the street's architecture. It was opposite a twenty-four-hour Laundromat covered in murals, including one of Minnesota congresswoman Ilhan Omar, and beside a 99¢ store selling Mexican prayer candles and bulk candy, up the street from a Chinese beauty shop brandishing a huge poster promising "after 30 minutes done, the much pretty full Eyelashes appear."

Inside the office space there were branded products in the bathroom, kombucha and rosé wine on tap in the common areas, and "community events" that included Cookie Friday. The offices were at less than 20 percent capacity, perhaps because you can't open the window without hearing the J/M line trains roar by just feet away from the first floor, or perhaps because Bushwick is a hard sell to tech start-ups and freelancers for whom the character of the neighborhood is important too. My guess is that hipster New Yorkers don't want to be asked for change by three different vulnerable-looking people before nine a.m., or they do want to know that their ideal types of coffee shops and bars are close by, and that they can easily meet their peers. I suspect the answer in Bushwick is not yet, but you can feel the change happening all around.

This is a neighborhood in flux, with a population that is 60 percent Latino and with a quarter of its residents surviving below the poverty line while under constant threat of displacement via gentrification. The De Blasio administration released its Bushwick rezoning proposal in April 2019. That came after the Bushwick Community Plan—a community-led rezoning proposal centered around preserving neighborhood character and avoiding displacement. The community put their plan together over four years, after watching development escalate and rising rents transform their neighborhood. According to *Gothamist*, there was contention between the city officials and the community during the presentation of the rezoning proposal. Winston Von Engel, the director of the Department of City Planning's Brooklyn office, stated, "Our intention is to preserve the character and the buildings, not the people in them."

The main streets have chain stores alongside Dominican barbershops, pawnshops, phone repair spots, and street vendors selling everything from three-packs of white T-shirts to fresh empanadas for $2 apiece. Mexican bakeries sit alongside independently owned restaurants like Yummy Chinese and Krazy Pizza & Wings. In a three-block radius there are two businesses that offer financial services to immigrants, like La Nacional, which advertises money orders, airline tickets, and flower delivery to the Dominican Republic. As is the case throughout many neighborhoods in New York City, Dominicans are the largest immigrant population in Bushwick. Maps of Ecuador and Mexico also fill the window of La Nacional, alerting the considerable populations of both communities to their services. I found one storefront particularly intriguing. Ecua Appliances, it's called, and it's stocked with refrigerators and ovens, with one corner full of crocheted cushion covers and ponchos. The proprietors, a middle-aged married couple, explained to me that the wife is an expert at crochet "in a Mexican style." I asked if she could make a baby blanket and she said she could have one ready in three weeks. I chose the colors and she told me it would cost $30 or $35. I offered to pay on the spot, since the wool alone would be at least $20. She wouldn't take any money, insisting she trusted me to come back.

On an empanada break one afternoon I passed by a striking building on Bushwick Avenue, taking up an entire corner. It was decorated like an Egyptian temple, with statues of pharaohs, paintings of ibis birds, and the eye of Ra adorning the walls. I asked a man sitting on a stoop a few houses away if he knew what the building was. He seemed a little cagey, speaking with a faraway look in his eyes. He told me the building was his place of worship. I asked what the name of the community or church was and he said that "things change." He asked me, if he was speaking to me twenty years ago, wouldn't I be different? We had to pause and nod solemnly at one another while a car lingered at the curb, blasting out the rap song "Face Down, Ass Up" at an extraordinary volume.

When the car pulled away, the man told me his community's name has now changed but they were known as Nuwaubians and he told me they used to own land in Georgia, which he was sad to lose. He told me not to believe everything I read about them. Later, I googled and read that the Southern Poverty Law Center described the Nuwaubian belief system as mixing "Black supremacist ideas with worship of the Egyptians and their pyramids, a belief in UFOs and various conspiracies related to the Illuminati and the Bilderbergers." In 2004 their founder, Malachi Z. York, received a 135-year sentence for child molestation and racketeering. The Bushwick building was their headquarters until 1983. It's a lot to take in, isn't it? I came across these layers of story in the space of half a block in one neighborhood, learning the bones of the narrative so far simply by speaking to one other New Yorker. There are 8.7 million of us, from all over the world and all over the country, and it's in the borderlands and the blends that the most fertile stories grow. Of course writers like myself want to write about the city, whether or not it cares to have its frantic history caught on a page. Such is the volume and the pace of change, I cannot even say that exploring the city, paying close attention and asking questions of it all, has helped me to understand it a whole lot more than I did ten years ago.

The smaller streets that thread between Broadway and the Ridgewood border, Cypress Avenue, are lined with well-kept terraced houses. Many of the houses are shingled and, judging by the number of doorbells at each front door, divided into three or more apartments. I saw a number of Puerto Rican flags, which makes sense if you know that almost one-third of Bushwick's Latino population is Puerto Rican. In a couple of cases the flags alternated with US flags on the same property, and in one case a black-and-white version fluttered beside the blue-and-red flag. This is the Puerto Rican "Resistance Flag" initially created by an anonymous artists' collective called La Puerta, to symbolize their wish for a nation independent of the United States. To the east, I walked through the Bushwick Houses, a New York City Housing Authority development, which, according to reporting by the *Brooklyn Eagle*, had the most murders of any public housing complex in the city in 2019. I saw nothing to indicate that level of violence, of course; I just saw some older kids looking after their little siblings, all of them playing in the fallen leaves and yelling for the sake of yelling, the way kids do. A variety of people waited for the bus, including a young family speaking in Spanish and an elderly woman dressed in an Andean style, with a heavy velvet skirt, a bright blue shawl, and a fedora.

As a subway hound I don't often take the bus, but it was the easiest way for me to get to Brighton Beach one afternoon in late summer. I took the B68 down Coney Island Avenue to get to the seaside neighborhood delineated by Ocean Parkway to the west and Manhattan Beach to the east. Right as we passed Neptune Avenue and I noticed the Al Mustafa Islamic Center of Brighton Beach, an old white man on the bus started to make a fuss. "That's not a toy. A bayonet, there, look! No wonder there's so much violence now." He was speaking loudly to a family seated opposite me: a mom in a pink salwar kameez and her two kids, probably around six or seven, with an older lady I thought must be their grandmother, wearing a burqa with everything but her eyes covered. The little boy had a plastic water gun, and that was making the old man irate. The old man wore a "Korean War Veteran" baseball cap and leaned on a walking frame. He kept repeating that the toy was a bayonet. The child's mother smiled and said, "It's okay—just a toy—plastic." She held it up, but that made him more annoyed. "You think this is a joke?" he asked.

I'm not sure if being a former soldier makes him more or less entitled to complain about toy guns; in any case, I sensed he was not annoyed at the family merely because of the toy. His companions were two elderly women who had been discussing their favorite doctors, a distinction seemingly based on availability. "Oh, Dr. Ratzinger is too busy these days, I don't bother with him," one of them said. Now their attention turned to the family. "Oh, look, one of them has a mask on," one old woman said, referring to the woman wearing a burqa, then she spoke louder to ask the mom, "Why don't you have a mask?" The mother replied, not hearing the question, "We are Muslim," and the old woman asked, sharply, "Why does she have a mask on?" The mom, deliberately or mistakenly avoiding the question again, said, "That's my mother-in-law." Nobody seemed particularly happy with the exchange, and the old white woman muttered to her friend, "Years ago the world was normal, you wouldn't see that. But now it's not normal." As ever, the word "normal" does a whole lot of work for those who deploy it.

Nearly two out of every three people living in Brighton Beach were not born in America. Eighty-four percent of the area immigrants are Ukrainians, Russians, and Uzbeks, so it's not surprising that Russian is the lingua franca. Along the main shopping strip I saw pharmacies, beauty shops, and law offices all offering their goods and services in Cyrillic script, sometimes with English translations written beside them. A Popeyes Louisiana Kitchen offering Cajun-style turkey faces competition from a number of specialty restaurants offering Russian and Slavic food. The entrance to Skovorodka is guarded by a life-size statue of a bear and has diner-style seating and heavy velvet curtains. The menu features borscht, eel salad, and komnot, a homemade Russian fruit punch. Walking toward the beach, I passed a busy restaurant called Euroasia with a menu reflecting its name. Options included typical central Asian foods like lulya kebabs and plov, a type of Uzbek rice pilaf.

In a *New York Times* feature, the writer Yelena Akhtiorskaya wrote about the changes she's seen in Brighton Beach. She moved there in the 1990s as a six-year-old, straight from Odessa to Little Odessa, as the neighborhood was known. Her parents were two of the thousands of Russian and eastern European Jews who escaped Soviet oppression by immigrating to this very spot in Brooklyn. Looking at the lunch options, I remembered what she had said about the place today. "It is the Central Asians who are now arriving in droves, rediscovering one another, molding the neighborhood according to their fantasies. A thriving Georgian community adds dimension to the culinary landscape. While Russian and Ukrainian food is delicious in its utilitarian way, it lacks the aromatic nuance of Georgian cuisine." I had initially wanted to get some khachapuri, that molten cheese bread they make in Georgia, and I read that Toné Café in Brighton Beach does a fantastic version. There is no imaginable scenario, no occasion that bread and cheese in any combination will fail to improve. They were out of khachapuri! I trudged across the street and got a sad iced coffee instead, from Dunkin' Donuts. The servers there were South Asian and wore headscarves; the clientele was largely Russian speaking and middle-aged, apart from one young goth man I couldn't quite place. Probably because the Underworld doesn't have a zip code.

It's quite a noisy neighborhood. The B and the Q trains rumble along an elevated track right down the main drag, Brighton Beach Avenue, and seagulls screech overhead. I walked toward the sea past a number of small clusters of people sitting out front of their apartment buildings. Most of the buildings looked more functional than stylish, and most of the people sitting outside were elderly; some were playing cards. One group of four old people sitting in wheelchairs and leaning on walking aids were chatting with a young mother, in a language I believe was Russian. The old people were doting on the child in her stroller and waved as the mother walked on. Another old lady walked extremely slowly ahead of me, carefully eating an ice cream cone she'd just bought from a Mister Softee van. Signs advertising (in both languages) an adult day care center called Garden of Joy and a home help agency called Welcome Care were prominent. The women all wore animal-print blouses and blinged-up flip-flops, big hair. They had tattooed eyebrows and plenty of lip liner, a look I find so fun and glamorous. The elderly men wore brightly colored swimming trunks and gold jewelry. *Just* brightly colored swimming trunks and gold jewelry.

I sat on the vast wooden boardwalk and watched as women in bikinis rinsed off their feet, and men in tracksuits and yarmulkes held deep conversation on a bench. The beach is long and wide and the sand is white; sailboats drifted past, families and groups of friends lay out and chatted under umbrellas. I squinted at the sea for a while and felt a bit too hot, but I kept my cardigan on because I hadn't thought to bring sunscreen. On my way back to the bus I stopped to pet a dog and noticed his owner's partner was wearing a T-shirt that featured the then president Trump as the Terminator, holding a gun and saying "I'll be back" with lots of small USA flags dotted around his head. I asked the man where he got the T-shirt, and he said, "Somewhere outside Michigan." That was only the second time I've seen someone wearing

Trump swag in New York City. I've seen it plenty outside the city—including small white children in "MAGA" baseball caps visiting, of all places, the National Museum of African American History and Culture in Washington, DC.

Taking my leave of the couple and their little dog, I remembered the whole reason I'd come out to Brighton Beach. I needed to buy some Russian nesting dolls for my niece's birthday. These are the kinds of tasks I really get caught up in and feel pleased about when I've completed. They are so much more concrete than "thinking" or "writing"—you either do them or you don't, and there is no equivocation or torment inside your head. I got the nesting dolls in a store called Kalinka, where they also sold T-shirts featuring Putin and Trump hugging each other. I wasn't sure if the shirts were meant to be worn ironically or not. I wondered about that as I walked back to the bus, past an outdoor market on the steps of the Oceanview Jewish Center. Two elderly women were selling tchotchkes and secondhand clothes, including big-shouldered fur coats the color and texture of foxes, the likes of which I've never seen for sale anywhere else. I didn't try on a coat because it was hot out. I was also quite nervous that, in the presence of these fabulous grandmothers, I'd so badly want them to think I was cool, I'd end up caving and buy my first-ever fur coat.

The majority of immigrant New Yorkers are naturalized citizens. There is also a large lawful permanent resident population as well as an estimated 560,000 undocumented immigrants. Approximately a million New Yorkers live in mixed-status households, where someone is undocumented. In the past few years under Trump, the nation's horrified eyes were understandably fixed on the Mexican border and the children sickening and dying in US custody there. I'd been watching too, and feeling terribly useless. That was one reason I decided to look closer to home, to see how my own city, thousands of miles from the border, is treating our most vulnerable immigrants: asylum seekers, the undocumented, those convicted of a crime. I discovered that life and death can hang in the balance here too, inside the big gray building at 201 Varick Street: immigration court.

Cases deemed sensitive are not open to the public, but technically anyone is allowed to observe some of the other court proceedings. Early on a weekday morning, I put on a blazer and waited in the hot sun for the building to open at eight a.m. Security guards opened the doors and let the first sixty people or so in to wait in line in the air-conditioned lobby. I chatted with an immigration lawyer I know a little bit—she's married to a friend of mine. She told me one of her former clients did the brickwork in this lobby, and was never expecting to find himself back in the building under threat of deportation, but that's what happened. That's what's been happening. To more and more New Yorkers.

The backlog in the immigration courts has been growing for the past decade, and pending cases increased by nearly 50 percent after Donald Trump became president. There are now more than one million people waiting for their day in court, many of them waiting for a judge to decide whether or not they will be deported. Around 5 percent of removal cases are based on a criminal conviction. The rest are civil immigration cases. They can include migrants arrested for crossing the border illegally, people who have overstayed their visas, and asylum seekers. The latter make up about half of new immigration cases in 2019, a record 159,590 cases. The Varick Street courthouse sees immigrants who are detained at US Immigration and Customs Enforcement (ICE) facilities in Orange County, Bergen County, and Hudson County. Normally these are immigrants who live in New York, but periodically asylum seekers from the border are sent to New York too, as was the case around a month ago.

One of the guards in the lobby seemed frustrated. "Move!" he shouted to a group of people confused about where exactly they were supposed to move. Then he muttered, "God, everybody is asleep. What is this, La La Land?" Surely he wasn't referring to the movie. There was far too much tension in that lobby for anyone to break into song. I get it; it's a tough job, shepherding overheated, nervous immigrants and the families of the detained.

In 2019, the number of immigrants being detained has reached a new high, and we know now about the horrific conditions many of them are held in. For those awaiting a court date, it seems gratuitous to even detain them in the first place. Most immigrants show up to their court dates. In 2016 the Department of Justice reported that "in absentia" cases—immigration cases for which there are no defendants present—stood at just 25 percent.

Unlike other courts, immigration court does not provide legal counsel if you're unable to afford it. Isn't that cruel? I know how complex and unwieldy the immigration system is; I've needed to call my own immigration lawyer in a panic more than once. I suspect that even more people, particularly non–native English speakers, would show up for court if they weren't facing the process alone. Nationwide, just 14 percent of detained immigrants have legal counsel. That's where my city shines. The New York Immigrant Family Unity Project (NYIFUP) is the nation's first public defender system for immigrants facing deportation—it's been funded by the New York City Council since 2014 and provides a free attorney to almost all detained indigent immigrants facing deportation at Varick Street.

Those attorneys, though? They are really up against it. I went through the X-ray machine and took an elevator to the courtrooms on the eleventh floor, run by the Executive Office for Immigration Review (EOIR), which is under the Department of Justice. It's strange, the place has the trappings and the feel of any other court but is not part of the judicial branch. The EOIR was created to oversee the courts in 1983; previously they were under the control of the Immigration and Naturalization Service, also under the Department of Justice. The American Bar Association, immigrant rights groups, and even some immigration judges have repeatedly asked for independence so they can stop being used politically, but to no avail. The administration controls the immigration courts.

I thought about that while I sat on a bench lining the back wall of the courtroom, next to toddlers wearing their hair in ribbons, staying as quiet as possible and waiting to see their parents, who filed in wearing orange jumpsuits, their wrists shackled to their waists. State and federal criminal courts also use shackles on defendants, but those are usually removed during trial to avoid prejudicing a jury. No such courtesy is offered to the immigrants. No matter why they are there, they stay shackled, unable to sit comfortably or wipe their face even as they recount the worst moments of their lives in their home country, asking for a stay of deportation, pleading for a chance to resume their life here in America.

The jumpsuits and shackles are certainly dehumanizing, but the immigrants that get to physically appear in court are the lucky ones. In 2019 ICE stopped bringing people from Hudson County and Orange County, moving instead to videoconferencing. Several legal aid organizations filed a class-action lawsuit in February challenging this move, and watching the proceedings I could see why. The man I saw onscreen seemed far away and tiny. Between having an ICE agent in the background as he spoke, and watching him strain to hear the translator through various technical glitches, it just didn't seem fair. The week I sat in, Bergen County switched to video too. The facility was put under quarantine after a number of immigrants contracted mumps there. And, during one of the hottest weeks of the year, the air-conditioning system in the jail completely broke down. When the pandemic hit, I thought immediately of immigrant detainees packed into prisons throughout the country. They were in grave danger, and the detention system actually became a vector for the disease. Deportees brought COVID-19 back with them to their countries of origin, and the virus spread quickly through detention centers. There were pleas from detainees, who even went on hunger strike, as well as joint appeals from thousands of physicians and from human rights organizations, detainees, and staff, who were infected at higher rates than the outside world. It got so bad that judges ordered ICE to release thousands of detainees with ankle monitors, and the number of immigrants in US custody actually went down for the first time in over a decade.

That morning I saw some judges treat immigrants humanely and politely, looking directly at them and explaining what was happening, wishing them luck before adjourning. I saw other judges treat immigrants like parts on an assembly line, to be dealt with quickly and moved along. But judges are operating within the rigid confines of immigration law, and they're under more pressure than ever before. Since October 2018 they'd had to work under a quota system, requiring them to "complete" seven hundred cases each year. If they failed, they faced negative performance reviews, which could limit their access to promotions and better benefits or even lead to termination. Judge A. Ashley Tabaddor, the then president of the National Association of Immigration Judges, told CNN, "It's another representation of the improper use of the court as an extension of the law enforcement policies of the executive branch."

When the Trump administration took children from their parents at the border between the US and Mexico, there was a huge outcry from American citizens and immigrants alike. Recordings of weeping children were released. The news out of Texas became difficult to bear, to know that there were children looking after babies and sleeping, hungry, on concrete floors. But when deportation could mean death, isn't indifference the same as cruelty? When President Obama declared he was deporting "felons not families," then banished a working father with a decade-old shoplifting conviction to a country thousands of miles from his American children, what else can we call that but family separation? A person who happens to be born elsewhere can have their rights stripped away in an American detention camp or an American courtroom. There is an entire machinery of brutality against immigrants in this country; some parts of it are new and shocking, other parts are quieter, though they've been there all along, even here in my beloved New York.

Later that week, I found myself in the Village again, looking at the menu of a hipster café with a $24 steak-and-eggs breakfast. Extraordinary to think that this place exists just around the corner from 201 Varick Street. "New York is peculiarly constructed to absorb almost anything that comes along," E. B. White wrote in "Here Is New York," and it does so "without inflicting the event on its inhabitant; so that every event is, in a sense, optional, and the inhabitant is in the happy position of being able to choose his spectacle and so conserve his soul." After leaving the Varick Street courthouse, I believe immigration court is a spectacle New Yorkers must choose to look at if we are to conserve our souls.

Later that year, I recalled the fur coats on sale out in Brighton Beach. I was feeling a million miles away from my body, which was cold and stiff and in need of a good shock. The most effective thing I know to do in that case is to take the F train to Herald Square and walk a couple of blocks to Koreatown, a tiny neighborhood that serves as the cultural center for the second-largest population of ethnic Koreans outside of Korea. When you're in the Midtown streets between Fifth Avenue and Madison, it's essential that you look up, and not just around, particularly along Korea Way, the densely packed and vertical heart of the neighborhood that runs along Thirty-Second Street. On a weekday at lunchtime I sidled away from the throngs of people and took an elevator to a spa over a bank. I was one of the only customers that afternoon. An eastern European woman sitting in the small reception area explained my options, and as she did I noticed a small sign that read, "Sometimes the most productive thing you can do is relax."

I was not about to relax, I was about to get scrubbed back to life. Open twenty-four hours a day, with women-only clients from nine a.m. to five p.m. on weekdays, the spa is laid out over two stories and it is not a place to be pampered. It's far more serious. I stripped in the changing room and took a quick shower. Then, wrapped in a towel, I went straight to the tiny, roasting-hot sauna. There was only one other woman in there that day, and while it is a little weird to chat to a stranger in a towel as you both gently cook, I imagine it's weirder not to. After that I sat naked in a plunge pool garnished with lemons like some kind of simmering fish fillet, then I was sent to the steam room by my technician, a middle-aged Korean lady with a commanding air. I hated the steam room, but I could feel my bones finally warming up, so I stayed as long as I could stand. Then I was instructed to lie on a plastic bed in a wet room, butt naked, so the scrubbing could commence. If you have never been scrubbed by an expert then it is impossible to understand how much better it is than exfoliating yourself. I apologize—I hate when people say that about experiences, but I swear, this is a completely different and almost incomparable experience to scraping off your own dry and dead skin in whatever piddling way you think is sufficient! The technician wears pot scrubber–looking gloves made from viscose and rayon. You can buy these mitts yourself, but again, nothing can replicate the skill and strength of these ladies. They go over every inch of your body in small circles, again and again, while layer after layer of your skin sloughs off in an enjoyable nightmare. I lay there, lifting various limbs and flipping over and back like an obedient seal, as she scrubbed and sluiced my entire body.

Over the sloshing water and sanding hands, the technician asked if I was going to see my parents at Thanksgiving. I explained that I'm Irish, and she said she's Korean so she does her own version of the holiday with her family. She said her kids, both in their twenties, had begged her to make their favorite dishes, so she had a lobster ordered and was going to pick it up after work at a market in Queens near where she lived. Then she told me at length how to make my favorite Korean dish, very basic and very delicious kimchi pancakes, and we both agreed at the end of the treatment that all this talk of food made us hungry. She pushed me into the shower—at that point my body was completely under her command—then yanked me out again. She then wrapped my baby-soft self in towels and told me to rest, so I lay in the salt room on a wooden bench and had one of the best naps of my life.

I was new, connected to the world again, and, bundled up in my winter coat, I spent the ride home smiling sleepily at a noisy bunch of schoolkids on the train. All of these places, all of these experiences, are waiting just up the steps from any subway stop. They're the arteries pumping people around the city's heart, keeping the city alive at the same time. In the dying days of the Trump administration, the

Department of Justice named New York City an anarchist jurisdiction, and I took a walk around my Brooklyn neighborhood. There was an old man in a plaid shirt leaning against the fence of the basketball court with his eyes closed, face turned upward in a beam of autumn sunlight. Perhaps he was enjoying a moment of solace with nature before winter, when we were all driven back indoors by the virus. Or was he gathering strength before smashing up the local Victoria's Secret and bringing home the lacy loot to his wife, most likely another senior citizen demented by lawlessness? A young woman pushed a stroller past me; she was clutching an iced coffee. Iced coffee when it's fifty-seven degrees out? Okay, chaos agent! Two women sat on a stoop, talking in low voices through masks; one of them was knitting. *Just like those French women watching the guillotine come down*, I thought, quickening my pace until I was halted by the city's notorious vandalism. A childish hand had scrawled, "don't step on the bees." Horrified, I threaded my way through some big yellow bumblebees chalked on the sidewalk.

Like most New Yorkers, I was exhausted by the Trump administration's bluster at that point, but I wanted to investigate this anarchist accusation a little further. I called Professor Robert Weide to ask if I was indeed living in a typical anarchist jurisdiction. He teaches a course on anarchist theory and praxis at Cal State LA, and turned down the volume on a kids' cartoon playing in the background before setting me straight. As it turns out, anarchy does not mean chaos. "Anarchists say that in a crisis, people revert back to what comes naturally to them, which is mutual aid." I suddenly recall, and tell Professor Weide about, a comedy writer I know who paid for one hundred haircuts for kids before school started after the lockdown. Another friend started a free book exchange in the corner of a city park. "Yup, that's all anarchism. All of that activity is based on an anarchist framework, whether the people who are practicing it know it or not." Even the term "mutual aid" comes from the title of a book written by Peter Kropotkin, a Russian anarchist and scientist much celebrated in the late nineteenth century. Kropotkin believed that competing with each other, or controlling and exploiting each other for individual gain, is not the wisest way to ensure the survival of our species. Rather, he proposed that humans actually stood a better chance of survival through protecting and cooperating with each other, and that is something we do naturally, without a coercive State controlling and patrolling our actions.

I looked again at my city. Anarchy sounds like neon-green hair, but our hair was gray. Gray because many of us lived through some of the most strange and frightening months New York has ever seen. Because we were too shell-shocked to step back into the salon to get our roots done.

Anarchy sounds like anger and, in truth, I was and still am furious that so many New Yorkers died because our government failed to protect us. When the virus came, it hit our city first and worst. Our teachers, bus drivers, and supers were left vulnerable and they were killed. The city was fed lies by President Trump, and we were left to fend for ourselves. Of course, this is not new for many New Yorkers who have been abandoned by the State, or were never included in the first place, and have to make do on their own. The city was strange in the summer of the pandemic—in all of that turmoil there was a gentleness here. Anarchy sounds like nihilism, like people don't care about the future or each other, but that wasn't how New Yorkers were behaving. They were growing zucchini on their fire escapes and checking in on their neighbors after a tropical storm ripped through the neighborhood. And what we did is not revelatory, according to Professor Weide. "When there's a hurricane, an earthquake, a tragedy, even people who are right-wing in their political beliefs come together in their communities and support each other and help each other. That's the epitome of anarchism."

When I think about the past few years, and who truly did give in to chaos and give up on empathy, it's not New Yorkers. The Trump administration was nihilistic, tearing up wildlife protection plans, sending asylum seekers away, beating up citizens on city streets. Professor Weide chuckled, then said, "I've joked to a lot of people that maybe Trump is actually a secret anarchist. He's dismantling American society, he's done more to dismantle American hegemony than any anarchist could ever dream of." Through bursts of laughter he says, "It's a supreme irony that the people destroying American hegemony are the people who think of themselves as American nationalists." It's certainly ironic, but I can't quite laugh about it.

A man did a terrible thing on a train once: he attacked two teenage girls. This happened in Portland, Oregon, in 2017. He was a white nationalist, and one of the girls was Black, the other in hijab. Then three other men on the same train did a beautiful thing: they stood up to the attacker and saved the girls. The attacker killed two of those men with a knife and injured the third. One of the men he killed was a gentle-looking twenty-three-year-old named Taliesin Myrddin Namkai-Meche. His last words were the most extraordinary words I've ever heard. Another passenger, who was trying to stanch his wounds, told reporters afterward that he said, "Tell everyone on this train I love them." Taliesin was dying, but he chose to use his final breaths to say that. For months I wondered: *who was everyone?* Did he mean the girls he saved, did he mean the other passengers, most of whom, understandably, did not try to physically stop the attack? Did he even mean his killer? All I know for sure is that everyone on the train was a stranger to him, but his last words were that he loved them. I try to hold on to those words. Love is an action: love is paying attention, love is a reckoning and a reconciliation with how the world really is. Somehow his words became a rule I made for myself: to try to better understand and accept this city of mine, to try to love everyone on this train.

Notes and Acknowledgments

Much of this book is memoir and much of it is reported and researched, so I'll list my sources here where I have not acknowledged them in the text.

I offer thanks to the artist John Byrne for discussing the context of his work with me and to Dr. Chioke I'Anson, who lent me his time and expertise on Richmond's past and present. The Irish blog *The Silver Voice* pieced together much of *Misneach*'s journey, and I'm grateful for their research and their generosity in publishing it. I consulted newspaper reports and city council archives for both Dublin and Richmond, and am indebted to the academics, public servants, and journalists who record history as it happens. For context and historical accuracy, as well as vivid storytelling that really brought this fascinating time in Ireland and America to life, I relied on both Dr. Maeve O'Riordan and Dr. Kara Hanley. I thank them both for their important work. Despite growing up in Cobh, I did not know how the island got her name until Felix Meehan, an archivist, explained it to me. Black Lives Matter has had a profound effect on my understanding of the country, and I thank the founders and members for this. I hope my relationship with the movement is not extractive; rather I aim to be part of it in my work and life. I am grateful too for the people I met in Richmond who generously took the time to help me think this piece through.

I'm indebted to Professor David Brotherton and Dr. Sarah Tosh for their dedication to exposing the intersections of criminal justice, drug, and immigration policy in this country, and for sharing that insight with students. The paper that led me to the expo is called "Proprietors of Death: An Ethnography of the 2019 Border Security Expo," written by Marianne Madoré and Nick Rodrigo and published in the book *Migration and Mortality: Social Death, Dispossession, and Survival in the Americas* from Temple University Press, edited by Jamie Longazel and Miranda Cady Hallett. A 2014 piece in *Politico* by Garrett M. Graff entitled "The Green

Monster" was a valuable resource for this piece. Similarly, reporting by Amanda Ripley (also for *Politico*) in 2017 entitled "Federal Law Enforcement Has a Woman Problem" helped me to understand the agencies I wrote about. I also gained insight from a 2020 article by Zoe Todd and Jodi Wei entitled "'Send Help': Inside CBP's Multi-Year Staffing Struggle" for PBS. For background on the phrase "boots on the ground" I relied on the late *New York Times* columnist William Safire, who figured it out with the help of an army historian.

Speaking of historians, Professor Mae M. Ngai's book *Impossible Subjects: Illegal Aliens and the Making of Modern America* is essential reading if you want to understand the origins of immigration policy in this country. For up-to-date reporting on the border and on US immigration policy in general, I consistently look to the work of journalists Caitlin Dickerson, Dara Lind, Alice Driver, Nick Miroff, Miriam Jordan, Hamed Aleaziz, Aura Bogado, and Jonathan Blitzer, to name just a few. I send my thanks and love to all journalists and migrants documenting the endless story that is human movement, as well as to the immigration organizations and advocates whose work I'm extremely grateful for.

Some of these essays started life as lines or whole

columns from my writing in *The New York Times* and *The Progressive*, so I'm delighted to express my gratitude to my editors at both places. Without their support and guidance I would not have been able to finish this book. So thank you very much, Max Strasser, Jenée Desmond-Harris, and Bill Lueders, as well as to the fact-checkers and copy editors who have made my work so much better along the way.

A 2003 Oliver Burkeman piece in *The Guardian* first noted the effects of the Luntz memo. Although I spend time on Luntz, he is the least interesting of all the "communicators" I mention. I hope, if you're not already familiar with their work on climate, you will seek out the writers George Monbiot, Rebecca Solnit, Eileen Crist, Robin Wall Kimmerer, and Glenn Albrecht. Much of their writing is available for free online but if you can, try to get ahold of Kimmerer's stunning book *Braiding Sweetgrass*. Huge love and thanks to the entire *Mothers of Invention* gang; it was an honor to work with each person I came across making that show. I will keep showing up for the work as best I can, because I know they will too.

Many thanks to the many friends, mentors, and teachers I leaned on to get this book written. To name just a few, I'm forever grateful to Emma Lee Moss, Mary H. K. Choi, Jack Tregoning, Negin Farsad, Nancy Foner, Richard Alba,

Kaitlin Mondello, Jon Ronson, Samantha Rose Hill, and my darling Meyer family. I would be lost without the really quite extraordinary Lindsay Edgecombe; thank you, Lindsay for being there come hell or high water. Many thanks due to Lindsay's lovely colleagues at Levine Greenberg Rostan too, particularly Monika Verma and Rebecca Rodd. My editor, Margaux Weisman, was unfailingly smart, kind, and wise. I'm lucky and glad to have landed on her lap. Patrick Nolan continues to support me and get me out of scrapes with grace and humor—thank you, Patrick! I'm besotted with the cover art and so grateful to Ilya Milstein for his talent and work. To everybody at Penguin Random House who mucked in to get this book done during a massively difficult time, with all of us working from home and scattered throughout the globe, thank you so much. I truly appreciate what you did. Thanks to my parents and my family, particularly all of the smallies, for being a constant source of love and inspiration.